# Mind Manipulation:

*Learn Beginners' Techniques for Mind Control, Mind Games, Mental Manipulation and Influence People, Defend Yourself and Recognize Emotional Control, Deception, Persuasion*

**Joe Silva**

# Table of Contents


Introduction.................................................................... 1
**Chapter 1: What is Mind Manipulation and Emotional Manipulation?**...................................................3
**Chapter 2: Why Do People Manipulate Others?**.........10
**Chapter 3: Mind Manipulation Techniques** ..............24

Mind Games........................................................24
Giving the Illusion of Choice ................................29
Intimidation.......................................................34
Bullying ............................................................38

   Bullying in relationships .................................. 40
   Bullying in the workplace.................................43

Altered Perceptions ............................................46
Social Pressure.................................................. 51

   Triangulation .................................................52
   Shaming and smear campaigns.........................57

Setting Time Limits ............................................59
Intentional Digression ........................................62

**Chapter 4: Emotional Manipulation Techniques**.......66

Victimization.....................................................66

   Common victimization scenarios .......................70
   Why victimization works..................................72

Playing With one's Emotions.................................73
Lying................................................................79
Guilt Tripping ...................................................84
Silent Treatment................................................ 88
Weakness .........................................................93
Dirty Looks.......................................................97
Voice Changes and Word Choices..........................100

Love Smothering................................................104

**Chapter 5: How to Recognize Mind and Emotional Control, and Deception**...................................... **108**
**Chapter 6: How to Defend Yourself against Mind and Emotional Manipulation**.................................. **120**

Know what you want ...............................................130
Stand your ground..................................................133

Realize that no one else can invalidate you .....................135
Make people respect and value your time....................135
Ensure that you always stay calm when you confront manipulators ........................................................136
Have specific expectations when confronting controlling people.................................................................137
Be patient..............................................................138
Ensure that you are transparent...............................139
Don't worry about coming across as selfish.................. 141
Timing is important................................................ 141

Be ready for the backlash .......................................142

**Conclusion** .............................................................. **144**

# Introduction

The following chapter will discuss the tricks and techniques that are used to influence people through mind manipulation and emotional manipulation. We will look at what manipulation means, and we will explain how it's different from other related concepts such as influence, persuasion, and even coercion.

We will look at the psychological reasons why people feel the need to manipulate and to control others. We will explore the dark personality traits that make certain people more likely to use manipulation techniques to their benefit. We will explain how sadists, narcissists, Machiavellians, and psychopaths are naturally more inclined to manipulate others.

We will also look at how people who aren't born with dominant dark traits can also become manipulative because of environmental factors and personal experiences.

We will thoroughly discuss mind manipulation techniques, and explain how they work, where they are likely to be used. We will also use real-world examples to illustrate how targets and victims react to mind manipulation techniques.

After that, we will thoroughly discuss emotional manipulation techniques. We will look at how manipulators can leverage a person's emotions to get what they want. We will look at the different techniques that are used to manipulate others in romantic relationships, friendships, family dynamics, and even workplace relationships. We will use real-world examples to help you understand how these techniques work.

We will also discuss how you can recognize mind and emotional control, as well as deception so that when someone tries to target you, he or she won't catch you off-guard. Finally, we will discuss techniques that can help you defend yourself and your loved ones against both emotional control and mind control.

There are lots of books on mind manipulation in the market right now, so thank you very much for choosing this one! Every effort was made to ensure that this book is filled with practical techniques and tips that can help improve your life, so please enjoy!

# Chapter 1: What is Mind Manipulation and Emotional Manipulation?

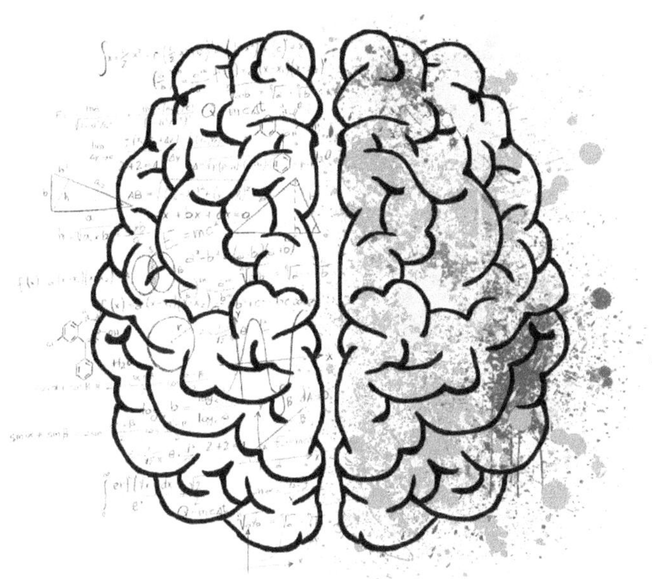

There are two ways to manipulate someone; you can attempt to change the way they think, or you can try to change the way they feel. The human brain is designed to process the world through thought or emotion.

In most people, one processing method is more dominant than the other; you can either be "more of a thinker than a feeler" or "more of a feeler than a thinker." In fact, in the conventional method that psychologists use to categories people into different personality types, people's inclination towards either thinking or feeling is one of the 4 main traits that's used to define different personality types.

Even though we tend to favor either thinking or feeling (as a construct of our personalities), the fact is that we all are highly capable of processing information in both ways, and the brain tends to choose the processing method that it thinks is appropriate under the prevailing circumstances.

For example, when dealing with a person that's close to you (e.g., your child, partner, family, close friends, etc.) you are more likely to process information related to them in an emotional way, but when you are dealing with casual acquaintances or strangers (e.g., your boss, a salesmen, a teacher, etc.) you are more likely to process information related to them in a logical way.

Irrespective of whether you process information emotionally or logically, your brain can be manipulated to increase your chances of arriving at a certain conclusion. When someone's feelings are manipulated, we call that "emotional manipulation," and when someone's thinking process is manipulated, we call that "mind manipulation."

"Manipulate" is a verb that means "to change by artful or unfair means so as to serve one's purpose." When someone sets out to manipulate you, they are trying to alter the way you think, feel, behave, or act, and they do it because the outcome benefits them somehow.

Manipulation is also referred to as "psychological manipulation." Psychologists think of psychological manipulation as "undue influence on a person or a group of people." That undue influence can be realized through "mental distortion" or through "emotional exploitation." When mental distortion is engaged, we call that mind manipulation. When emotional exploitation is engaged, we call it emotional manipulation.

Mind manipulation techniques, as we have said, are those that distort the way a person thinks. These techniques work by either reducing a person's ability to think in a logical or critical way, or by changing the beliefs, values, attitudes, and assumptions that a person makes when he perceives certain things.

We fall for mind manipulation techniques because our belief systems are altered, and as a result, we truly believe the assertions that the manipulator is making at the moment.

Emotional manipulation techniques, on the other hand, play with the way a person feels towards either the manipulator or other people that the manipulator is leveraging. We fall for emotional manipulation techniques either because we want to please other people, or because we want to prove something to them.

Mind manipulation techniques are methods of influence that disrupt people to their very cores. They alter the very things that a person uses to define himself; they can change his identity.

When mind manipulation techniques are effectively deployed, they can temporarily give a person a new outlook (this true in cases of milder forms of mind manipulation such as mind games) or they can completely overhaul a person's very identity and replace it with a new "pseudo-personality" (this is true in cases where extreme forms of mind manipulation, such as brainwashing are used).

Emotional manipulation techniques, on the other hand, are methods of influence which change a person's "emotional priorities." They alter the way the subject feels towards a specific person, relative to the way he or she feels about himself or herself, or other people.

When a person uses emotional manipulation against you, you feel a sense of obligation to do what they want because you are emotionally invested in their wellbeing, or because you are afraid of certain emotional consequences that you'll suffer if you don't do what they want.

In both mind manipulation and emotional manipulation, the manipulator takes advantage of the trust that's is bestowed on him or her by the victim.

In relationship dynamics, that trust can take the form of affection. You are more susceptible to manipulation from people who you hold in high esteem: it could be a man or woman you are sexually attracted to; it could be a boss who you have a professional obligation to respect; it could be a charismatic leader whose ideas you like.

For any kind of manipulation to work, there has to be some common ground between the victim and the manipulator. So, in a way, manipulation can be seen as a violation of trust.

Mind and emotional manipulation also take advantage of a person's good-natured. "Good people" are more susceptible to manipulation than "bad people." If you are a person of goodwill, a fair-minded person, you are more likely to trust people implicitly, to give them the benefit of the doubt, and to indulge them even when they make you uncomfortable. That's because your brain operates under the premise that people are generally good; even if you suspect that a person has an ulterior motive, you'll still go out of your way to treat them with decency and to be considerate towards them.

Everyone is susceptible to mind and emotional manipulation. It's easy for you to assume that you are too smart to be manipulated, or that you are too emotionally stable for someone to play with your emotions, but that's a myth that we should dispel from the very beginning of this book. No one is too smart to be manipulated. As long as you have thoughts and feelings, someone can manipulate them.

If you are very smart and unfailingly logical, someone can use a well thought out logical argument to convince you to behave in a certain way. If you feel strongly for the people in your life, those people (or other third parties) can use those feeling to control your behavior.

The worst thing you can do is assume that only foolish or careless people get manipulated. You too can be victimized by a manipulative person, through no fault of your own. To protect or defend yourself against manipulation, the first thing you have to do is acknowledge the fact that you are vulnerable to it.

Most manipulation techniques out there utilize both mental and emotional aspects, so it can be difficult to distinctly categorize certain techniques as either mind manipulation techniques or emotional manipulation techniques. Sometimes, the way we think and the way we feel can be closely intertwined in such a way that it becomes impossible to unlink them.

One such technique is the manipulation of facts. When someone manipulates facts, they are messing with both the way you think and the way you feel. So, manipulation of facts can be seen as both a mind and an emotional technique.

That explains why many popular psychologists don't bother making the distinction between the two. Most of them lump all manipulation techniques together because they believe that at the end of the day, manipulation is manipulation; it doesn't matter if it's mental or emotional.

I don't buy into that argument. I believe that the distinction is important because it helps you to understand the working mechanism of each manipulation technique, and the better you understand all techniques, the more likely you are to triumph over the machinations of the manipulative people in your life.

# Chapter 2: Why Do People Manipulate Others?

In everyday conversations, it's common for people to use the words manipulations, influence, and persuasion interchangeably, but these words have different meanings.

The reason why people confuse these words is that in some scenarios, there can be an overlap between, say persuasion and influence, influence and manipulation, or manipulation and persuasion. It's important for us to clarify the meaning of each of these terms.

Influence is defined as the power to change or to affect a person or an object. This power enables the "influencer" to cause certain changes, without forcing those changes to happen. So, influence can be consciously detected, or it might happen on a subconscious level.

Another characteristic of influence is that it reveals very little effort from the "influencer" and sometimes, he or she might, in fact, be unaware that his or her actions are influencing someone else.

Persuasion is defined as the act of causing one or more people to believe something, or to take a certain cause of action. Persuasion often involves direct communication of some kind. Persuasion and influence can be interchangeable at times (especially where the intention of the persuader or the influencer are clear and deliberate), but unlike influence, persuasion almost invariably requires intent.

You persuade someone by making what you want clear to them and then using certain words or certain actions to sell them on the idea. When you influence someone, you can take the time to make your intentions clear, but oftentimes, others may just be influenced by watching your actions or listening to your words. For example, a child may be influenced by his parents just by watching the way they conduct themselves.

Manipulation is defined as influencing someone using shrewd and devious techniques with the intention of benefiting oneself. Unlike regular influence and persuasion, manipulation involves subverting a person's will. It involves tricking a person either by playing with his/her emotions or by messing with his/her mind with the explicit intention of taking advantage of them.

It's important to mention the term coercion because it's sometimes used interchangeably with manipulation. Coercion is indeed a form of manipulation, but it's unique in the sense that the shrewd and devious techniques that are involved are forcefully deployed.

In coercion, threats and physical force may be used to get a person to act or behave in a certain way. Coercion is illegal, and in some cases, a violation of people's basic rights, so it's rarely used in ordinary relationships (people want to take advantage of others, but not many of them are willing to go to jail for it).

Now that you understand what manipulation really is in the context of other related terms, let's look at the reasons why people manipulate others.

We all have a desire in us to feel like we have control over something. We want to feel like we have dominion over our lives, our futures, our careers, and our surroundings. That's just how the human mind is wired. When we feel a sense of control over our lives, we feel mentally secure.

We want to feel like things aren't just happening to us. We want to know that we are at the steering wheel and that we have a say in what direction our lives are taking at any given time.

People manipulate others because they lack a sense of control over certain aspects of their lives, so they try to control others to satisfy that innate need for control. When people feel that their ability to control certain situations is slipping from them, they make an effort to reassert that control.

Psychologists have established time and again that people who feel like they have no control, compensate by trying to control others. In fact, sometimes the reactions that a person exhibits from the realization that he has lost control over something can double as manipulation techniques. When you lose control over your emotions, for instance when you get angry, and you express that emotion, the person on the receiving end of that emotion will be influenced by it, and it will affect the way he acts or behaves. When you feel like your relationship is falling apart, and you react with jealousy, that jealousy will influence your partner by making him or her either defensive or subservient.

Subconsciously, people reason that if they can control another person, then they are in control. Even if that person has nothing to do with whatever's out of control in the first place, it doesn't really matter.

For example, a guy who spends the whole day getting yelled at by his boss in the office may feel like he has no power or control. However, when he gets home, he in turn bosses around his wife and his children, and that feels oddly satisfying to him; it makes him feel in control again.

Logically, he knows that his controlling behavior is misplaced, and controlling his family is not the same as controlling his work, but that doesn't matter. To him, it's a release. His stress and anxiety had been piling up, and it had to be released somehow. What's worse, that feeling he gets when he unloads his stress on other people is somewhat addictive, so once he does this for the first time, it easily turns into a habit.

Some manipulative people seek to control others because they lack empathy. Most people have empathy, which means that their brains are wired in such a way that they are able to relate to the way others feel. They can put themselves in other's shoes, and they can understand that their actions are harmful to those people.

The ability to empathize with others can be gauged on a spectrum. You either have high, medium, or low levels of empathy. Manipulators generally have medium to low levels of empathy (they fall on the lower end of the spectrum).

Manipulators tend to have dark traits such as narcissism, sadism, Machiavellianism, and psychopathy. These dark traits are responsible for most of the antisocial behavior that lots of people exhibit. Just like empathy, all of these dark traits are present in everyone to varying degrees.

The higher someone rates on the spectrum for one or more of these traits, the more likely he or she is to manipulate someone else for his ow her own gain. Those people who rate the highest for these traits are more likely to push the furthest when they are manipulating others.

Sadists have a dark trait called sadism, which psychologists define as a tendency to inflict harm on other people for one's own pleasure. Originally, sadism was thought to be a trait that only existed in the criminally insane, but psychologists came to discover that it is actually a trait that exists in regular people; the kind of people you encounter every day.

All people have the potential to be sadistic (it's a trait that lies dormant in all people, and it can be awakened by certain personal experiences). If you have a friend who tends to be perfect all the time, and then something happens so that he or she is taken down a peg or two; you will feel a certain level of satisfaction, even if you know that your friend is having a bad day.

That is a sign of latent sadism, and if it's nurtured (due to growing up in a bad environment with a lot of emotional turbulence), you could find yourself resenting other people's happiness, or even actively trying to make them unhappy.

Sadists manipulate others, not because they want something concrete from them, but because they just want to see them suffer. When others suffer, they enjoy it. They would seek to hurt other people physically, emotionally, or even sexually.

When they meet people who seem vulnerable, they are excited by the prospect of inflicting pain on them. To them, it's not about settling a score; it's just about intentionally hurting or humiliating someone else. Sadists tend to be very angry, and they are highly likely to resort to physical violence if their machinations don't work on a person they are targeting.

Narcissism is a dark trait that gives people a sense of entitlement. Most manipulative people tend to have relatively high levels of narcissism. Many people confuse narcissism with having high self-esteem, but there is a clear difference between those two things.

People with high self-esteem value themselves, and they value other people as well. Narcissists, on the other hand, believe that they are inherently better than others, so they manipulate others as a way to reinforce that belief.

Narcissists don't see others as equal to them, so they don't care about their feelings or their welfare. They tend to have a grandiose sense of self-importance. That means that in their minds, they truly believe that the way they feel is more important than the way everyone else feels. They'll lament when you hurt their feelings, but when they do the same to other people, they won't think for a second that it's a big deal.

Narcissists believe that they deserve to have other people serve their interests. Some of them believe that if you do something that benefits them and harms you, it's okay because, in their minds, their comfort is for the common good; after all, they are special. They believe they deserve to have you attend to them hand and foot.

Narcissists also manipulate people because they have a deep-seated need for love an admiration (they don't give it; they just expect to receive it). They want you to hold them in awe and to praise them all the time. If you don't, they may manipulate you to make you do it. They expect favorable treatment wherever they go.

When they get into relationships, they genuinely believe that they are more important than the people they are dating, and they feel as though they are doing the person a huge favor just by being with them. So, when you are in a relationship with a narcissist, and you don't do everything he wants you to, in his mind, you are taking him for granted, and you deserve to be punished for it.

Narcissist lack empathy for other people, and they are completely oblivious of how others feel. When they enter into friendships and other kinds of relationships, it's never really out of love; they just think that they have found someone who can be subservient to them and give them anything they want.

They may also get into relationships because they think those relationships help their public images; they'll want to be with an attractive woman or a powerful man so that everyone else sees that they are truly superior.

When narcissists manipulate and seek to control others, it's never really personal. When they target you and put you through emotional turmoil, it's never really about you. They may be charming and charismatic, but it's almost always a fake emotion, intended to deceive people and to earn their trust before the manipulation begins.

Machiavellianism is a dark personality trait that is dominant in people who are good at coming up with complex schemes to manipulate others. While sadists manipulate others in order to enjoy their suffering and narcissists do it to show that they are better than others, Machiavellians manipulate people because they want something very specific from them. They manipulate their coworkers because they want to advance in their careers. They manipulate the public because they want to gain power.

Machiavellians believe that in whatever they do, the end justifies the means. With that line of logic, they can rationalize any kind of manipulation. They won't hesitate to use people or even to deceive them to get what they want.

They are particularly good at concealing their true intentions, and they may come up with diabolical plans that span months or even years. They hold their cards close to the chest, so it can be extremely difficult for you to tell if they harbor ill intent against you. They'll show their true colors when it's too late.

Machiavellians are cold and calculating, but they tend to have lofty goals, so they are unlikely to manipulate people for petty personal reasons. That means that Machiavellians may not be particularly dangerous in romantic relationships.

However, their one shortcoming in relationships is that they lack passion, and they tend to fake affection. They also have a very utilitarian outlook, so they could easily discard any relationship if it doesn't serve their purposes anymore.

Women with the Machiavellian trait can turn out to be "social climbers" (those who get into relationships in order to climb up the social ladder) or "gold diggers" (those who get into relationships for economic reasons). Men with the Machiavellianism trait tend to think of their female partners as trophies (symbols of success or status), or they too can use women to climb up the social ladder.

Psychopathy is the worst kind of dark personality trait that one can have. Psychopaths completely lack empathy, and they don't have a conscience. They may also have one or more of the other dark traits that we have mentioned so far. They are totally selfish, and they are completely callous. They don't care about the rules and norms that govern our societies. They don't ever worry about ethical codes. They just do what they want.

Most people are ruled, not just by a fear of consequence, but by an internal moral compass that helps them tell the difference between right and wrong. That moral compass is what we refer to as a conscience. Since psychopaths lack a conscience, they don't see things as either right or wrong. They are completely amoral. They just do the things that make them feel good. They don't get into relationships because they are looking for intimacy; they do it for sexual gratification or to fulfill some other superficial needs.

When you encounter a psychopath, he or she won't think of you as someone to be treated with consideration. To him or her, you are one of two things; a means to an end or an obstacle on his or her path. That kind of callousness allows them to do things that are extremely predatory.

Psychopaths often end up professions where success is inversely proportional to conscientiousness (areas such as politics, high finance, sales, etc.). Since they have no qualms about harming others, some of them become con artists, serial philanderers, or even hardened criminals.

Since psychopaths lack empathy, they don't feel the way others do. However, they are very good at feigning certain emotions when they want something from you. They can be charming, and they can convince you that they are in love with you. Once you have fallen for them, they can subject you to unimaginable levels of cruelty.

Apart from having a need for control, and rating highly on the dark traits that we have just looked at, manipulators may also be motivated by their own past experiences.

There are certain things that can happen in one's life, which leave him or her emotionally scarred, and as a result, he or she feels the need to manipulate others, either as a way of compensating for that damaging event or as a way of preventing the same thing from happening again.

Take the example of a young woman who enters a relationship with a charming young man. She gives her whole heart to him, and they seem perfect together by all indications. After investing two years in that relationship, she finds out that the guy is cheating on her.

She breaks up with the guy, and she is heartbroken. Once she is over that relationships, she meets a different guy, who also seems nice by all indications. She starts a loving relationship with him, and he seems to really care about her as well.

However, when he starts coming home late, she can't help but refer back to her past experience. She feels like the same thing is happening all over again, and she feels like she must do something to prevent it. So, she becomes controlling.

She starts monitoring his messages, making a fuss when he receives calls late at night and subjecting him to interrogations when he doesn't come home as early as she expects.

When the man asks her to trust him or to respect his personal boundaries, she can't get herself to do it, so she tries to manipulate him further by guilt-tripping him.

In this case, the young woman in question is not narcissistic, sadistic, Machiavellian, or psychopathic. She is just a normal person who has insecurities. She becomes manipulative, not out of malice, but because she feels that it's the only way for her to hold on to her relationship.

# Chapter 3: Mind Manipulation Techniques

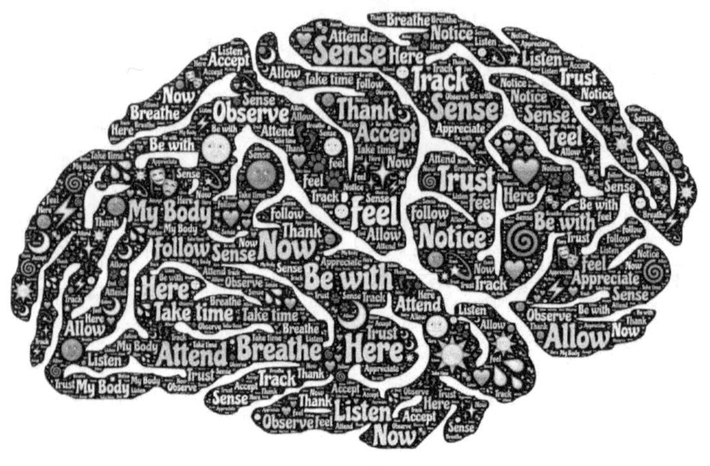

As we mentioned in the beginning, mind manipulation techniques work by influencing the way a person thinks, or the way he perceives certain situations. These techniques are created to alter a person's ability to think critically so that he can opt to process thought and to act in ways that benefit the manipulator. Let's take a look at 8 of the most common mind manipulation techniques out there.

## Mind Games

Mind games are highly versatile manipulation techniques because they come in many different forms; any manipulator can invent his own midgames based on the strengths or weaknesses that he perceives in his target. Mindgames can be defined as subtle attempts to control someone (whether it's through the use of words or actions).

Although mind games are primarily designed to trick the mind, they also work by leveraging people's emotions. They are extremely common in relationships and other social dynamics. They aren't always deployed with malicious intentions (for example, parents often play mind games with their kids to get them to do what's in their own best interests, and sometimes, spouses use mind games to get their partners to take actions that are mutually beneficial for the both them).

Here, we will discuss the more malicious kinds of mind games; the kinds used by manipulators to exert control over their victims.

Malicious people, especially sociopaths, often use charm as part of their mind games. They approach their targets and win their trust using the "charm offensive." To such individuals, the ability to charm people is an important skill which they spend lots of time sharpening; they groom themselves to look nice and attractive to their targets. They even practice smiling in front of mirrors.

Charm works because people like to feel flattered. When people are on the receiving end of the charm offensive, they feel special, and they let their guard down. That is when the manipulators get them hooked.

Manipulative people (particularly the sociopaths and psychopaths) are very good at appearing cool even when they are under pressure. That is part of their charm. For instance, when such manipulators are juggling multiple partners, and they receive a call from one partner while they were with the other, they take the call, talk calmly, hang up, and make up a plausible story about who was on the other end of that call, without breaking a sweat.

In manipulation, charm and glibness go hand in hand. Manipulators use the most flattering terms to describe their targets, fooling them into thinking that they are in love with them. All the flattery leads even the smartest targets to ignore their gut instincts and to fall for the manipulators' machinations.

People also play mind games by indicating no remorse when they are at fault. Usually, in a relationship, when you catch someone on a lie, they'd own up to it and ask to be forgiven. However, that's not the case with some manipulative people.

Such people may decide to push back with a mind game that is carefully designed to turn the tables and to convince you that you are the one who is at fault. People who use this sort of mind game are extremely comfortable with lying, and they generally lack empathy towards others.

Manipulators may also show indifference towards you or the concerns that you raise with them. When they express indifference towards you, manipulators are trying to shift the power balance in your relationship in their favor. After initially charming you, and after you have grown accustomed to their affection, they'll suddenly withdraw and start acting like you are just an acquaintance, no more special to them than anyone else. You'll try to regain that special feeling by doing things that you think are pleasing to them, and that's when they'll gain control over you.

Manipulators also like to use confusion as part of the mind games they play with their victims. They can confuse you by twisting words and turning them in their favor, as they try to pull one over you.

They may say something but then later claim that you misunderstood them, or they may outright deny ever saying such a thing at all. they may open up to you in private and admit to having certain fears to make themselves seem vulnerable, but once you have decided to give them some consideration, they'll go after you in public, and turn you into a sucker.

One other mind game manipulators like to play is the blame-game. This is where they literary make everything your fault, and you are forced to act defensively all the time. If they are eloquent or savvy enough, they could even manage to convince you that you are the unintentional instigator of the problems that they clearly caused.

People who play mind games like to cite analogies and metaphor as evidence to support their manipulative claims. Because most of the assertions they make are fabricated, they never have real-world evidence for them, so they make up metaphors.

These metaphors are usually highly sensationalized, and they often make for bad advice. If they are trying to get you to abandon your principles, they'll give you a rousing speech, full of metaphors about exercising your freedom and reclaiming your power, and that way they'd convince you to do the craziest and most damaging things, to their benefit.

So, how do you know that someone is playing mind games with you? The first sign is that they always want to know every detail of your life. To them, information is power, and the more they know about you, the more effective their mind games will be.

You may also be able to notice that they are testing you to see how you will react under different situations. Mind games are only effective when the manipulator has a general understanding of which buttons to push when they want to mess with you, and the only way for them to know this is by testing you.

Also, if you pay close attention to the way they act in the early stages of your association with them, you may notice that they have a subtle air of superiority about them. People who play mind games tend to think of themselves as smarter than their targets, so even when they are hiding their true nature in an attempt to charm their targets, putting them in a situation where they feel their intelligence is challenged can force them to reveal just how superior they feel.

## Giving the Illusion of Choice

The illusion of choice is a mind manipulation technique were the manipulators' limits the options at the victims' disposal in a subtle way so that when the victims make their choices, they do so while still believing that they are exercising their free will. This technique may also involve the manipulator coming up with ideas and finding ways to convince the target that it was their idea all along.

Everyone loves having free will. People like to have a choice in matters that concern them; they are happier when they feel that they can make their own decisions and that they are in control of their own lives.

Manipulators, on the other hand, seek to control their targets' lives, which essentially means that they are trying to get their targets to act against their own free will and better judgment. That puts the manipulator and the target on a collision path because, before one of them triumphs, there has to be a battle of wills.

However, even the weakest targets still tend to have a fairly strong sense of free will, so manipulators understand that their chances of winning in such instances are very minimal. That is where the illusion of choice comes in.

We tend to think of choice as our ability to make decisions when there are two or more alternative courses of action in front of us. That understanding of the concept of choice is wired deeply into the way our mind works. If someone offers you one option, you are going to wonder if there are any alternatives for you to consider. However, if the same person offers you a handful of options, you are going to compare those options and select the one that is most suitable for you. It might never even occur to you that there could be other possible options other than the ones that have been set in front of you.

Manipulators understand this behavioral tendency, and they use it against people all the time. In fact, the illusion of choice is used by major companies to sell consumer products to customers, who end up buying them under the assumption that they are exercising their free will. When you are shopping at the supermarket, and you want to pick up a box of cereal, you might see dozens of options on the shelf, each with a different product and brand name; you might even compare the products, and select the one that you think offers you the best nutritional value, and you will go away, satisfied that you made the right choice. What you might not know is that all those products and brands are probably manufactured by the same parent company. That, in a nutshell, is how the illusion of choice works on a macro scale.

In interpersonal relationships, manipulators use the illusion of choice by asking questions that are carefully designed to produce specific answers. For example, if you are dating someone who is controlling, instead of asking you "Where do you want to go for tonight's dinner date?" they'll ask "Do you want to go to restaurant A or restaurant B?"

In your mind, you will start weight the two options, and you will pick one of them. This works best in cases where the manipulator does his homework and carefully selects a target who is generally agreeable.

The examples we have talked about cover scenarios where the manipulators are okay with the targets choosing from more than one of their hand-selected options. However, there are certain cases where manipulators want to restrict the target to just one possible option, but they still want the target to have the illusion of choice.

In such cases, they'll present the target with two or more options, but among those options, only one would be logical or truly viable.

Let's take a possible example from the workplace. A manager has to hire one new employee. He asks his assistant to look at the profiles of several candidates and shortlist the good ones. The assistant manager is controlling and wants to usurp his boss's authority, so he decides who he wants to hire.

He then finds a few other terrible candidates for the job, puts their profiles together with that of his preferred candidate, and presents the list to the boss. When the boss reviews the choices he is given, he may think he is choosing from a pool of viable candidates, but it turns out, the decision was already made for him.

Sometimes, manipulators can offer their targets one reasonable choice and one hyperbolic choice so that their targets end up choosing the option the manipulator wants while still maintaining the illusion of choice. Even when the other choice is marginally worse than the one the manipulator wants you to select, you may still feel like it was your choice after all.

For example, a controlling boss could tell you to either stay a couple of hours after work on Friday to finish your project, or to come in during the weekend. Since coming in on the weekend sounds marginally worse for you, you will take the two extra hours on Friday because it seems like the more reasonable option.

The illusion of choice makes you forget that you are still getting the short end of the stick. That's because of the way it's presented, it makes you feel that the situation could be a lot worse, so you take the better option and count yourself lucky.

The illusion of choice can also be used in interpersonal relationships to make someone feel like the choice they have to make, in fact, a foregone conclusion, so they are forced to move forward (as the manipulator wishes) by making a choice.

# Intimidation

Intimidation refers to words or actions that manipulators use to cause other people to fear harm or injury. It's used by manipulators to instill fear in their targets so that they comply with whatever demands the manipulator is making.

For the manipulator, the point is to convince the target that resistance is futile. Effective intimidators are those who are skilled in expressing emotional tenacity and resolve; that's because intimidation only works if the target is convinced that the manipulator is really determined to follow through on whatever threat he is making.

Intimidation works because it throws the target off-balance, and it puts him or her on the defensive. Intimidation can be covert or overt, but in either case, it serves to weaken the will of the victims to assert for themselves, so that they clear the path for the manipulators to have things their way.

When intimidation is used overtly, it often involves the manipulator engaging the victim in a deliberate and intense confrontation, where every threat is laid out in the open. The purpose here is to challenge the validity of whatever issue the victim might be complaining about, to make sure the victim feels that his way of looking at things isn't even legitimate or acceptable to the manipulator.

Overt manipulation involves a great deal of posturing on the part of the manipulator as a way of asserting dominance over the target or victim.

Overt intimidation is used by manipulators in arguments to counter what the victim is saying. For instance, when a victim asks a manipulator to do something he promised to do, the manipulator may deny ever making such a promise. If the victim keeps insisting on his claim, the manipulator could get up (to make himself appear physically dominant), stare down the victim and demand to know, "Are you calling me a liar?"

Just by doing this, the manipulator could get the victim to back down. This often works when there is a power disparity between the two people. It could be that the manipulator is physically stronger than the victim, or that he outranks the victim in the social hierarchy (like in the case of a boss versus an employee or a teacher versus a student).

On the other hand, covert intimidation is a lot more subtle. Instead of spelling the threat out loud, the manipulator will either imply it or use nonverbal signals to indicate it. The manipulator could use certain gestures, throw certain glances at the victim, use specific facial expressions, stare down the victim, glare at him, or even use a shrug with the intention of intimidating the victim.

This mostly works in cases where manipulators and victims are well acquainted with each other, and the victim has developed a certain intuition about the manipulator's emotional state. By seeing the nonverbal signal that the manipulator puts out, the victim knows that if he or she continues with a certain course of action, there is going to be hell to pay.

People who use intimidation tend to rank highly when tested for traits such as narcissism. They want to control people and make them do as they wish, but they are afraid of being challenged on an intellectual level. They know that they either lack the intelligence or the moral standing to get the outcome they are looking for, so by intimidating others, they are doing everything in their power to keep their victims from challenging them one on one.

Another way that manipulators intimidate their victims is by bombarding them with questions, often in an angry tone. When they do this, they don't wait for the victims to respond; they just keep throwing question after question, until the targets get overwhelmed and decide to back down.

These questions can be critical, accusatory, and extremely personal. In some cases, the manipulator will choose a line of questioning where he makes leaps that indicate that he is deliberately misunderstanding whatever point the victim is trying to make. Since the victim is trying to have a mature discuss, he will be limited by the laws of logic, so he'll find himself trying to clarify his position, or even trying to apologize for being misunderstood even though the manipulator knows full well what he really meant.

Your brain is wired to consider open hostility as a form of threat, so if you are trying to reason with someone and he keeps firing hostile questions back at you, your fight or flight response kicks in. If you decide to fight back (i.e., if you start using intimidation against the other person), you lose your moral high ground, and you sink to their level. If you choose flight (i.e., if you back down) the other person wins by default). So, intimidation works well because wherever it's used, there is very little upside for the victim.

Intimidation is a logical and emotional quicksand; you can't reason with the other person, but you also can't fight back without losing.

Part of the intimidator's strategy is to overwhelm the victim with his intensity. That means that when you meet someone (for example in the early stages of a new relationship), and you notice that he is really intense, it could be a sign that he likes to use intimidation to get what he wants.

# Bullying

Bullying is defined as a distinctive pattern that involves causing harm to others or humiliating them so satisfy one's own psychological needs. Bullying is different from mere aggression. For harmful actions to qualify as bullying, they have to be deliberate and repeated.

Bullying is a durable behavioral style that people tend to pick up during their developmental stages. Bullies start out as children, but many of them grow out of it. Those who remain bullies in adulthood do so because they always got what they wanted from bullying others, so it never occurred to them to change their behavior. Children who bully others are more likely to outgrow their bad habit if they face some kind of reckoning (for example, if they victimize someone who fights back).

Psychologists believe that bullies generally lack pro-social behavior. Compared to the rest of the population, they are less likely to experience anxiety. The end result of this is that they fail to comprehend the way others feel. That's partly why they are so insensitive to others, but it also explains why they are particularly dangerous manipulators.

Bullies feel a need to control others, but they are not good at reading other people's emotions. They often misinterpret the intentions of others, to the extent that they sometimes interpret neutral situations as hostile.

Bullies may have positive views of themselves, but they worry that others don't see them the way they want, so they impose themselves on others in an attempt to control the way they are perceived. For example, they might think of themselves as strong or smart, so the reason for their aggression towards others is to prove that they indeed have these traits.

Bullies need victims. Without victims, they don't feel complete. They are also very particular when it comes to selecting their victims. They look for weak people who are unlikely to assert for themselves. For them, such people are fairly easy to spot because they radiate fear, even in situations that are generally non-threatening. A bully can easily pick a potential target from a crowd, just by observing their body language and general demeanor.

Bullying is more of a mind manipulation technique than an emotional manipulation technique because the objective of the bully is not just to oppress people and assert dominance over them, it's to brainwash them and to control the way they think about him.

## Bullying in relationships

Manipulators use bullying in interpersonal relationships and even in professional relationships. In relationships and marriages, bullies tend to think of their partners as their own person stress relievers. Bullies will find spouses or partners who they know have reservations about fighting back.

A man might look for a woman who grew up believing that women ought to be subservient to their husband, or one who is too much of a lady to get into verbal exchanges with him. A woman, on the other hand, might look for a man who is laid back and passive.

When the bully gets stressed at work or by any of life's challenges, he or she comes home and unloads on his or her spouse. For the bully, it's about spreading the pain around, and for the victims, it's a life full of unpredictable horror.

Sometimes, people bully others because they themselves are bullied by other people, and so to them, bullying is kind of restorative (it gives them a semblance of control over their own lives, or at the very least, it dissipates their pent up anger).

Psychologists have found that people who were bullied by their own parents growing up are more likely to bully their spouses or even their children. This is a phenomenon called "rage of generations." The idea is that if you had (or still have) parents who were critical of your choices both as a child and as a young adult, you start perceiving the choices you make in your life through their eyes, and can sometimes find yourself criticizing those choices (in yourself or in others) the way your parents would have.

Manipulators bully their spouses and partners through name-calling. They often used negative names and labels to indicate their frustration or to convey their anger. These can be profane names, or they can be the kinds of labels that are meant to belittle their victims and make them feel either inferior or subservient.

Bullies also taunt their targets, particularly when they gain the courage to push back against the bullying. This is done to ensure that their targets remain under their control, and they are discouraged from acting in their own best interests. For example, if a victim tries to tell the bully to stop, he may say things like "Or else what?" or "What are you going to do about it?" to make the victim feel helpless and hopeless.

Bullies in relationships also tend to get verbally and physically aggressive. They may go on verbal tirades, criticizing their partners for every little thing as a way to vent over the stress from other aspects of their lives.

In some cases, bullies can get physical, or they may act in ways that convey threats of physical violence. In rare cases, bullies may even escalate to the point of aggressive sexual behavior, where the aggressive party uses sexual violence as a way of asserting dominance over the other person (you may have heard of instances of rape within marriages or stable relationships).

Bullies also tend to exhibit controlling behavior over their partners in relationships. They point here is to deny the victim any sense of freedom or autonomy. The end goal is to make the victim feel like he or she only exists to serve the interests of the controlling person.

Controlling behavior is often accompanied by put-downs. In this case, the bully will keep telling the victim how he or she is doing everything wrongly, and the result is that the victim feels the need to prove to the bully that he or she can do better.

If you are an outside observer, it can be easy to tell if someone you care about is in a relationship with a bully. That's because bullies like to put down their victims in front of other people. A bully will tell his or her spouse's secrets to other people, and he or she will twist the facts so as to embarrass his or her spouse maximally.

Those who bully others in relationships often do it to cover for their own feelings of inadequacy, or they do it because they are egocentric and they don't care about their partners.

## Bullying in the workplace

Bullying is extremely common in the workplace, and unlike in relationships, it isn't always thought of as a vice. In fact, there are some careers where the ability to bully others is thought of an asset (people like lawyers and law enforcement officials have core job functions which they can only fulfill by bullying others). However, even in such professions, bullying between colleagues is generally frowned upon.

Manipulators in the workplace use bullying to get under other people's skin, to throw them off balance. The fact that most institutions have rules that govern inter-personal relationships doesn't mean that they have policies against bullying. In fact, most workplace bullying doesn't meet the threshold of what most companies consider to be harmful. In lots of companies, bullying in the workplace isn't even outlawed.

Studies show that the majority of workplace bullies are in positions of authority. Most of them are usually managers and bosses, which means that's it's almost impossible to eliminate systemic bullying problems in most organizations.

Manipulators bully others in the workplace through aggressive communication. This is where they make public scenes around the office, with the aim of instilling fear in the people they are targeting, as well as everyone else that may get in their way. These kinds of bullies are known for getting into loud altercations in the office, sending out angry and strongly-worded emails and memos, and using aggressive body language cues to intimidate people.

Manipulators also bully their colleagues at work through constant criticism. They always find something negative to say about their colleagues, no matter how hard they work. These bullies tend to be in managerial positions, and sometimes, they may criticize others because they are afraid of being surpassed by their juniors (so they refuse to acknowledge that their juniors are any good at what they do).

For some bosses, bullying is also a way of getting maximum productivity out of their subordinates (some managers believe that constant criticism puts employees on their toes). Their criticisms are often dished out in public when the target's colleagues are watching so that it can be more embarrassing and demeaning.

Manipulators may also bully their colleagues by denying them access to certain information or resources that they need to be able to perform some of their job functions. These bullies act as gatekeepers to certain resources in the office, and the fact that they control those resources gives them a sense of dominance over others.

For example, some bosses may give their subordinates assignments, but fail to give them the proper instructions on how to complete those assignments; this gives them the perfect opportunity to criticize and belittle them when they inevitably underperform.

Some manipulators may also bully others in the workplace by meddling with them behind their backs. They may make up rumors about their target and turn their colleagues against them. They may also do it to undermine a person so that they can be thought of as incompetent or lazy. This is usually done by manipulators with traits such as Machiavellians, who are in direct competition with their targets (for example, the two of them may be eyeing the same promotion).

Manipulators in the workplace often feel emboldened, and they get away with their machinations because they generally tend to be top performers in their jobs. In fact, studies show that workplace bullies tend to do well in areas such as sales and other fields that are characterized by high levels of aggressiveness.

# Altered Perceptions

This is arguably the worst kind of manipulation that anyone can be made to endure, and it's usually practiced by the worst kinds of manipulators. Most garden-variety manipulators will seek to take advantage of others for their own benefit in various ways, but only the more hardened manipulators (mostly sadists, narcissists, Machiavellians  and especially psychopaths) will go so far as to try to alter someone's reality.

Manipulators who alter others' perceptions generally lack a conscience. They completely lack empathy for their victims, and they don't have the ability to connect with people on a human level. They can't bond with others and make friends. They enjoy it when others suffer, and it makes them feel either strong or aroused.

Manipulators of this caliber won't hesitate to hone in on a person's good nature and take total advantage of them. In fact, they think of positive human traits as weaknesses that they can exploit, and they do it with much delight and enjoyment. When they get into someone's life, they latch on in a parasitic way, and they use and abuse the person without any compassion or compunction. They use sophisticated brainwashing and reality-altering techniques to keep their targets under their influence.

Altering someone's perception involves the use of gaslighting and brainwashing. Gaslighting is more common in romantic or close personal relationships where one person has psychopathic tendencies. Brainwashing, on the other hand, is more common in impersonal but controlling relationships, and it may be used on more than one person at a time (for example, cult leaders are able to brainwash entire congregations).

Brainwashing and gaslighting both involve overwhelming or overpowering the victim's senses in such a way that they lose touch with the internal guidance systems that define who they are. Brainwashing can get someone to let go of their most important beliefs and values, while gaslighting can make someone lose trust in their own objective view of reality.

Manipulative people tend to constantly challenge their victims thought patterns and values, to the point that the victims lose track of the thoughts and values that make up their personalities. When the victim's internal guiding systems are broken, and they don't know who they are or what they believe anymore, there is a void that is left, and the manipulator will be ready to step in and fill that void.

The end result is that the victim will put the manipulator at the forefront of their own conscience so that their whole life will be about the manipulator.

Manipulators also alter their victim's reality by creating a sense of paranoia, which causes the victims to be hyper-vigilant. Once they are in a person's life, manipulators will start abusing the target's perspective, by being extremely critical of it.

If you have a belief system in place, they'll insult that belief system at every chance they get, until the victim becomes uncertain about it. If the victims have certain weak areas (maybe they have low self-esteem, or they are self-conscious about certain aspects of their lives), manipulators will hone in on that, and they'll open those wounds over and over until the victims totally doubt themselves.

With time, victims will get to a point where they can no longer tell right from wrong. Since abuse is a constant part of their lives, they'll no longer be able to tell that it's a bad thing, because it will literally be their new normal.

When the victim can no longer make judgments about what's right and wrong, the manipulator will start to regulate the victim with their moods and their needs. This is what psychologists refer to as "emotional dysregulation." The victims' sense of right and wrong will be guided by the emotions that are reflected back to them by the manipulators. So, if they do something, and the manipulator reacts with a hot temper, then it registers in their brainwashed minds that the action is negative. If they do something and the manipulator seems pleased by it, then that becomes a good thing in their minds.

Manipulators also use neurolinguistics programming techniques to alter their victims' perceptions and to make them doubt their own feelings and experiences. For the victims that are being exposed to neurolinguistics programming techniques for the first time, it can feel as though the manipulators have telepathic abilities (that partly explains why people who are brainwashed by cult leaders tend to think of them as divine figures with supernatural abilities).

Experienced manipulators will study their targets, read their body language, and predict their behavior in a way that leaves the targets in awe of the manipulator, and completely scared of doing anything to assert for themselves.

These kinds of manipulators tend to target people who are good-natured and have no suspicions about the manipulators' intent, let alone extent of the evil that the manipulator might be capable of. In fact, most victims fall into manipulators' traps because they are just trying to connect with a fellow human being, and they innocently attempt to accommodate the other person's idiosyncrasies.

The more the victim accommodates the manipulator, the more he sinks his hooks into her, and the harder it is for her to break from his control. In fact, many victims never realize that their perceptions are being altered until it's too late.

Manipulators who use perception-altering techniques often start out by concealing their intentions until they have earned the trust of their victims. For an external observer, it can be easy to assume that the victims in such cases are gullible individuals, but that couldn't be further from the truth. The fact is that even the smartest and most assertive people can have their perceptions altered if they find themselves under the thumb of a master manipulator.

When such manipulators identify their potential targets and meet them for the first time, they'll use love bombing techniques to make the targets feel special. Love bombing involves intense and regular displays of affection, and it may include sending flowers and gifts, taking the target to lots of fancy places, giving them as much attention as possible, and flattering them through verbal compliments and romantic messages.

Love bombing increases the odds that the target will fall in love with the manipulator at a faster rate. It also ensures that the target doesn't take the time to really analyses the manipulator and discover possible red flags. Love bombing also keeps the target from seeking feedback from her support system (since she is so head over heels, in love with the target, she may disregard any warnings that she receives from her friends and family).

Psychologists understand that gaslighting and brainwashing can only occur with the consent of the victim; the manipulator will push the victim's personal boundaries, and with every small concession that the victim makes, he or she loses a little bit of control to the manipulator.

Mental health professionals have also discovered that the loss of control over one's reality can occur in a sort of domino effect. When the manipulator pushes the victim's boundaries, and she cedes a little control, the next time he pushes again, it would be much easier for her to cede some more control because it's something she has already done before. And as time goes by, it becomes a norm. Before she realizes it, the manipulator would have pushed so far, that she would be miles away from reality.

## Social Pressure

The use of social pressure to influence others is fairly common. Companies use social pressure to sell products all the time; people make decisions every day based on how they think other members of society are going to perceive them. Manipulators, however, take it a lot further. They use social influence and social pressure to make their victims feel helpless and force them to comply with some of their other manipulation techniques.

There are several types of manipulation techniques that work primarily because they are characterized by social pressure. The manipulators are aware of the fact that people care about appearances and their public reputation, so they'll leverage that to get potential victims to do what they want. Although there are plenty of social pressure techniques out there, we will focus our discussion on two of the most common ones; triangulation, and shaming (which includes smear campaigns).

## Triangulation

Triangulation is a learned behavior than many people use to influence other members of their social circle, but manipulators often use it with deceptive and malicious intent. It is common in dysfunctional relationships, families, friendships, and even among colleagues at work.

In triangulation, manipulators will identify good-hearted people who care about the opinions of their friends and family, and they'll bring social pressure to bear in order to manipulate them. In this case, when the relationships begin, manipulators will use love-bombing to win over, not just the target, but also the people in the target's inner circle.

For example, a manipulative man won't just try to seduce the woman he is targeting; he will try to charm her friend and to get close to her family so that everyone thinks that he is a great and lovable guy.

Psychologists define triangulation as a form of indirect communication, where the communicator pretends to be the messenger between two other people. In other cases, it can be seen as a direct form of communication, where the communicator tries to get someone else to be his or her accomplice so that they can "gang up" on the primary recipient of the message. The communicator is usually the manipulator, the primary recipient of the message is usually the target, the accomplice is usually the mutual friend who is blind to the intentions of the manipulator, and the message is always carefully crafted to serve the manipulator's agenda.

Now, let's look at a few methods that are used in triangulation.

The first and perhaps the most common method of triangulation is one that involves "killing two birds with one stone." In this method, the manipulator will try to get positive attention from the target by claiming that a third party did something that was potentially detrimental to both the manipulator and the target.

For example, a manipulative boyfriend may tell his girlfriend that one of her friends was flirting with him. Now, this will accomplish two things.

First, it will make the girlfriend jealous and insecure; she will feel like she is replaceable in that relationship. As a result, she will start working harder to please the manipulative boyfriend because she doesn't want to lose him.

Secondly, this will create animosity and distrust between the girlfriend and her friend, and a rivalry between the two might spark. If the manipulator is a narcissist or a sadist, he might just enjoy the conflict between his girlfriend and her friend because it gives him a sense of power or satisfaction. However, if it's a Machiavellian or even a psychopath, there may be a bigger plan at play; it could be that he is trying to put a wedge between his girlfriend and her close friend so that their bond is severed, and she no longer has the social support systems that she currently enjoys (it's easier to exploit someone when she doesn't have many people to turn to).

The second type of triangulation is the kind that involves recruiting reinforcements with the intention of bringing the pressure down on a target. This form of triangulation is often used in family dynamics and some other relationships, without any malicious intentions. For example, as a child or a young adult, when your mom wanted to convince you to do something, and you were resistant, she would probably rope in your dad, your siblings, and even your grandparents and she'd get them to tell you the same thing.

Manipulators use the same technique, but it's different because they'll twist the truth in their favor. If the target has a different opinion or belief about something, and the manipulator wants to change it, he will get unwitting third parties to help change the target's mind. He will approach the third parties and feed them his version of events (he'll often use lies of omission to convince the third parties that the target is wrong), and then he will invite them to confront the target over the matter.

The people who are brought into the conflict often have no idea what the real story is, and they may just think they are trying to help by giving their objective assessment of the situation.

In some instances, it could be that the manipulator is a well-respected member of the social circle to which he and the victim belong, and everyone else who doesn't know his true nature holds him in awe. He could be the friendly neighbor who treats everyone with warmth, but then abuses his partner behind closed doors; people will readily believe his side of events, and they'll rally to his side and help him by piling social pressure on his spouse.

This kind of triangulation may work for two reasons. The first reason is that the target may feel that being negatively perceived by her social group is worse than just conceding, so she'll give up and agree with the manipulator. The second reason is, she may think that if everyone else sees the situation from the point of view of the manipulator, maybe they are all right, and she is the one who is wrong.

The third method of triangulation involves the manipulator putting two people in direct conflict with each other. He will smear the character of one person in front of another one, and then swear the listener to secrecy. He will then turn around and do the exact same thing with the other person.

In relationship dynamics, one person may be the target, and the other one may be collateral. However, when this plays out in the workplace, both people could be targets, and the manipulator (usually a Machiavellian in this case) will be hoping that they'll destroy each other and pave the way for him to triumph.

In some cases (particularly in dysfunctional relationships) the manipulator may even cast himself or herself as the victim to gain the sympathy of a third party as he or she pits the third party in direct conflict with the real target (in this case, his or her partner).

After manipulators have taken advantage of their targets in toxic relationships, and they are ready to break up with them and move to their next targets, they can use a triangulation technique call "pre-discard and dump" to end the relationship and to make sure they come out on top.

In this technique, the manipulator will confide in members of the social circle about his intention to break up with the target, making it extremely clear in the process that the target is the one at fault. The manipulator may do this in advance (several months or even years before the actual break) so that by the time the target knows there is an impending breakup, everyone would have chosen the manipulator's side, and she would be left isolated, with no social sympathy or support.

## Shaming and smear campaigns

Shaming and smear campaigns may be used as an independent influence technique, or they may be used as part of any of the triangulation techniques that we have discussed above.

Shaming involves using the fear of social disapproval to strong-arm someone into acting in a certain way.

As social creatures, we all want to be perceived positively by the people around us, and manipulators can use that desire against us in many different ways. Shaming is a particularly effective control technique, and it comes in many forms.

Manipulators can publicly shame you through sarcasm, expressions of disgust, and name-calling. They can also use your sense of shame against you by asking you to do certain things in public, in front of others. It becomes much more difficult for you to assert your point of view with an audience present, especially if they make it seem as though you are the one who is selfish or controlling. You might just say "yes" to keep everyone else from thinking of you as the bad guy.

Smear campaigns refer to instances of manipulation where the manipulator goes around saying negative things about the target behind his or her back. As we have seen above, it is used in almost all triangulation techniques.

The purpose of a smear campaign is to preemptively damage the reputation of the target with members of the social group so that when he or she tries to seek their support, later on, everyone will already think of them as the pariah, and they won't readily listen to their side of the story.

# Setting Time Limits

Some manipulators control their targets and victims by setting time limits for them, or by convincing them to agree to certain timelines.

Now, ultimatums and time limits are used every day in all kinds of relationships, and they aren't necessarily bad things. For instances, parents use time limits to get their kids to do their chores, or bosses can give time limits to their employees to increase their focus and productivity. Employees use time limits to assert themselves in order to get fair wages and favorable working conditions.

However, time limits and ultimatums in romantic relationships are always problematic because they involve leveraging a person's love or affection. That can be a source of serious contention, even when the person setting the time limit does it with good intentions.

In business situations, manipulators use time limits to create a sense of urgency in the person they are targeting. Such manipulators aren't necessarily malicious; it could be a real estate agent trying to get you to buy a house by claiming that it will be out of the market by the end of the week. It could be a salesman trying to get you to make a purchase before a certain discount offer expires. It could also be a recruiter trying to get you to take a certain job offer before the position is filled.

The idea here is that you will act fast out of a fear of losing out, so you'll make a rash decision that benefits the manipulator. Companies use time limits all the time to instill the "fear of missing out" in their potential customers, thus forcing them to act immediately.

In personal relationships, time limits may be used in the same way. For example, if you a person tells you to choose whether or not you want to be with them, and he gives you a small window of time within which to make your decision, he is counting on the fact that due to the pressure of the time constraint, you won't be able to objectively assess the merits and demerits of the choice you are about to make, so you are more likely to make a decision based on emotion rather than logic.

There are many different kinds of ultimatums that manipulators use in romantic relationships. Manipulators who use ultimatums are usually hedging their bets, so they'll use other forms of manipulation to make sure that the target likes them enough to comply with the terms of their ultimatum.

Usually, manipulators may test their targets by giving them small ultimatums, and when they get what they want, they'll keep raising the stakes in subsequent requests, until one day, they ask for the thing the really wanted.

When setting time limits or ultimatums, manipulators may say things like "If you really loved me, you would do this" or "If you don't do this by this time, I'll know that you don't love me." This is a form of emotional blackmail because it turns compliance into proof of affection.

Manipulators can also ask their targets to give up on their values for them; they'll ask you to act in a way that is contrary to your core principles, as a way of proving how important they are to you.

Manipulators will also threaten to leave you if you don't do what they want. As far as ultimatums in relationships go, threatening to end the relationship is as high as the stakes go, so they'll first make sure that you are heavily invested in the success of the relationship, or you are in a mental state where you are informed by a deep fear of being alone, before they ask what they really want from you, and present you with the ultimatum.

For all intents and purposes, ultimatums and time limits are threats. The target acts out of fear of the outlined consequences, and not out of a conviction that they are making the right call. This means that when a target concedes and agrees to meet the manipulator's timeline, he or she loses control over his or her own life, and opens the floodgate, letting in more time limits and more ultimatums.

## Intentional Digression

The term digression refers to a rhetoric technique where a person diverts from the topic at hand. Traditionally, digression was used as a way of making a bigger point about the topic that was originally under discuss; the orator would divert and talk about topics that seemed unrelated, but towards the end, he would circle back and link his narrative back to the original topic, revealing the bigger picture in the process. Manipulators do something similar, but they mostly use digression to serve their manipulative agendas.

When you are having a conversation with a manipulator, and he feels threatened, he may digress by projecting his shortcomings onto you. when a manipulator sees that you are bringing up a topic which is going to make him look bad, he will jump ahead and accuse you of the same thing that you were about to accuse him of so that you are stuck on the defensive, and you are unable to address the core issue. Projection is similar to "blame-shifting," which is a mind game where the manipulator tries to convince his victim that he or she is the one who is at fault.

In some cases, digression can take the form of a nonsensical conversation. When the victim confronts the manipulator with the intention of having an open and honest conversation, the manipulator will counter by taking in a way that is objectively nonsensical; he will use word salads (where words are thrown around in a way that they give off vague assertions, but there are no coherent ideas that are being communicated).

The manipulator may also turn the discussion into a circular conversation (where you keep going back and forth on the same issues instead of making actual progress in the conversation). He may also turn the conversation into a personal attack (where his argument is directed against you personally, instead of being directed counter to the ideas for which you are arguing).

Manipulators may also digress by making generalizations or blanket statements instead of taking the time to listen to properly, and address the specific issue that the victim is raising. If for example, the victim asks the manipulator to stop doing something specific, he could accuse her of "nagging" him and dismiss the issue outright.

Generalizations and blanket statements are a sign of "intellectual laziness," and the people who use these digression techniques are afraid that if they discuss an issue point by point, they won't come off looking smart or reasonable, so it's better for them to dismiss the issue outright.

Manipulators also digress by deliberately misrepresenting people's assertions. This is where they understand the point that a person is trying to make, but because they are trying to avoid having a frank and mature conversation, they'll go to absurd extends to pretend that they have misunderstood the other person.

If you tell them, "Please stop doing this because it's bad," they'll respond by saying, "So you are saying in a bad person?" They'll pretend that their feelings are very hurt, and you might find yourself consoling or reassuring them instead of standing firm and addressing the issue at hand.

Sometimes, the manipulators may also digress by completely changing the subject. They'll try to take the conversation in a whole other direction, preferably one where they are viewed favorably. In social discourse, this is sometimes referred to as "what-about-ism." When you talk about an issue, the person counters by saying, "What about the other time when you did..." The manipulator will use any of the victim's past transgression to keep from talking about their own present transgressions.

Manipulators also digress by using the "pre-emptive defense technique" to keep themselves from being held accountable for anything. When they sense that the target is about to criticize them, they'll start listing all their positive traits and explaining why they are the "nice guy," and how after all the good they have done, they deserve to be trusted. The victim may then feel awkward about bringing up the controversial topic, and she may just let things go.

# Chapter 4: Emotional Manipulation Techniques

There are very many different emotional manipulation techniques that are used by both well-meaning and malicious people to influence others. In this chapter, let's discuss 9 of the most common emotional manipulation techniques which are often deployed by manipulators, in romantic relationships, friendships, work relationships, and even among family members.

## Victimization

Victimization is perhaps the most complex emotional manipulation technique because it entails so many different things. There are very many different methods that manipulators can use to victimize others.

Technically, all forms of manipulation can fall under the umbrella of victimization because they involve taking advantage of people, and getting them to do things that aren't in their own best interest, or forcing them to settle for conditions that are unfavorable for them. Let's look at victimization as a concept, and explain how it works, why it works, and what it looks like in everyday situations.

For victimization to occur, it primarily requires two people; a victim, and a victimizer. However, to the outside observer, it's not always clear who is who. In fact, in many cases, victimizers use diabolical techniques to convince the victims and even third-party observers that they are in fact, the ones that are getting victimized. This is more likely to happen in cases where the victimizer prefers covert manipulation techniques, than in cases where the techniques chosen by the victimizer are mostly overt.

The term victimization refers to the acts and the processes that come into play when a person is being turned into a victim by someone else. Victimization entails both psychological machinations and physical action.

The most common forms of victimization are bullying, physical abuse, peer victimization, assault, verbal abuse, and sexual abuse. Some forms of victimization are more closely associated with certain segments of the population than others, but it doesn't mean they are unlikely to occur in the general population.

We tend to think of victimization as only occurring in cases where there is a power imbalance between two people, and that the more powerful person is the one who's always the perpetrator, but that's not always the case. Sure, in physically abusive relationships, the stronger person is often the abusive one, but in psychologically abusive relationships, the situation can be a lot more complex.

Of the various forms of victimization we have mentioned, verbal abuse is the most common non-physical form. It occurs in all sorts of dynamics (romantic relationships, families, friends, and even among colleagues). All sorts of victimization have psychological consequences, but for our purposeless, we will focus mostly on the "manipulative" forms of victimization (including verbal abuse) rather than the "criminal" forms of victimization (such as physical abuse and sexual abuse).

We've mentioned that it can be hard to tell who's who in an abusive relationship if you are an outside observer, but perhaps it can be easier to tell if you are able to identify the symptoms of victimization. When a person is victimized, he or she might end up showing signs of anxiety and depression and may express feelings of being trapped in an abusive relationship. However, the person may also feel as if he or she has no other option but to stay within the abusive relationship, so he or she will start "rationalizing" the abuse and accepting their "lot in life" as a victim.

One thing that psychologists find fascinating about victimhood is that it is paradoxical. When people are victimized for a prolonged period of time, they get to a point where they become comfortable with being victimized, and they choose to stay victims instead of seeking help or standing up for themselves. When a person endures trauma as a result of victimization, especially during their earlier developmental stages (in childhood), they can develop what's known as the "victim mentality."

Your earlier experiences have a way of programming you to take certain roles in dynamics that involve victimization. In fact, it's not victims alone who get programmed; depending on your formative experiences, you could be programmed to be a victim, an abuser (a perpetrator), or even a bystander.

If you were abused in your formative years, as an adult, you might subconsciously seek out abusive relationships. If you witnessed others getting abused in your formative years, and you felt powerless to do anything about it, there is a high likelihood that you'll turn into a "bystander" when you witness abuse, even if you are an adult who can take action.

Manipulators have a way of identifying people with "victim mentality" and people with "bystander mentality," and they know exactly what to do or say to manipulate both kinds of people.

So far, we have talked about victimization in terms of abuse, but as we mentioned earlier, all forms of manipulation result in victimization. Let's look at various other ways that manipulators victimize other people:

## Common victimization scenarios

A manipulator could make vague promises about doing something that would help a or benefit the victim at some point in the future, then, based on that, he or she would ask the victim for something substantial in return, at the present moment. If you understand the principle of reciprocity, you know that human relationships are governed by a mutual sense of "give and take." By promising to "give" in the future, the manipulator gets to "take" at the present moment, with no intention of ever living up to his promise of reciprocation.

A manipulator may also make a unilateral decision on behalf of a victim, knowing full well that his action is not in the best interest of the victim. When a manipulator wants to control your life, he could make major life decisions on your behalf because he understands that "it's easier to ask for forgiveness than permission." No matter how much you protest, it will be after the fact, and the decision the manipulator makes will, in some cases, be irreversible, and all you can do it accept it and live with it.

Manipulators could also leverage the things that are owed to you to get you to do what they want. These could be things that you are entitled to, but you need their help to access them. In some cases, they might even be basic necessities which they are responsible for providing to you. They could also threaten to sabotage opportunities that you have if you don't give them what they want. In other cases, they might leverage your standing in the community by threatening to sully your good name with false claims unless you comply with their requests.

Manipulators may also victimize you by wearing you down, to a point where you just give up on fighting them. Let's say that you are trying to negotiate on something, with the aim of making a joint decision that is mutually beneficial for both of you (as partners do in relationships). If the manipulative person notices that you won't agree to something that he wants, he suggests that you table the discussion for later. However, from that point on, he'll keep coming up with new concerns and conditions that force you to give up your stand on the matter.

## Why victimization works

Victimization tends to work best when it's dished out in small doses. The person would first work to earn your trusts so that you let him into your life. Once he is in, he will keep working on getting close to you, until he gets to a point where he has considerable influence over your life.

As a psychological manipulation technique, victimization is mostly used by people who are in your life, not by strangers. That's because for victimization to work, the person has to have the power to turn the emotional screws and make you bend to their will.

So, when you meet a person for the first time, and he is charming, you can try to figure out if he is a victimizer by looking at the way he treats the people who have been in his life for much longer than you.

## Playing With one's Emotions

Manipulators are experts at playing with other people's emotions. They understand that emotions are indicators of people's deepest motivations, so, once they are aware that you feel a certain way about something, they are going to use that against you to get what they want.

If what you want is to be with them (like in the case of romantic relationships and marriages), they could manipulate you by making access to them contingent on your compliance with the requests that they make. If what you want is something that's extrinsic to you (for example, in career situations, you may want a promotion), they could also find ways to get between you and your dreams, and then leverage them against you.

A well-practiced manipulator can take advantage of pretty much every emotion that you are capable of expressing. If you feel guilty about something, the manipulator could use that against you. He or she will frame the situation in such a way that giving them what they want is the only way to prove that you are truly sorry about what's transpired.

The guilt doesn't necessarily have to be valid or based on something that was your fault. As long as they can get you to feel the slightest guilt about something, they could leverage you by making you feel the need to atone for that guilt.

Manipulators can also play with your emotions by taking advantage of your ego and making you feel that you have something to prove to them. We all have pride in us, and we fear "losing face" especially when others are watching, so manipulators can get us in a bind by taking us into doing things we don't want to do; we feel obligated to comply with such requests because we are worried about how others are going to see us.

As far as emotions go, pride is one of the most irrational ones. Because of pride, we can end up harming ourselves just to show others what we are capable of; we all do this to some extent to impress people. However, when a manipulator sees this side of you, he will keep raising the stakes, until you feel forced to take on a risk that you aren't willing to shoulder.

Manipulators can also play with your emotions by taking advantage of your sense of duty towards him or her. When the people in your life need help, you can't turn your back on them; you have to do everything in your power to help them because you are a nice person. However, manipulators can hold onto that sense of obligation that you feel towards them and take advantage of you, and abuse your help.

In as much as we help others, it's unhealthy to keep helping if it causes us to suffer. Manipulators will want you to give up on your own needs in order to attend to their needs. They'll want to co-opt your life to the extent that your priorities become secondary to theirs.

This happens in all kinds of relationships and interpersonal dynamics. If someone did a favor for you, they could leverage that to make you feel like you owe them forever. Even an ailing parent could manipulate you into letting go of your own career and relationship prospects in order to take care of him or her.

The fear of rejection is a common emotion that manipulators love to play with. The use what psychologists call "emotional blackmail" to force people to do what they want? The way it works is that the person gets you to do what they want by constantly threatening to detach from you if you don't comply.

In romantic relationships, the person will threaten to break up with you in order to control you. You will find yourself in a position where you constantly have to prove your love for the other person by doing exactly what they want. If you don't comply, they'll tell you that it's a sign that you don't love them, and that they don't see the point of staying in a "loveless" relationship.

Manipulative people can also play with your emotions by taking advantage of your sense of gratitude towards them. If they do you a favor, they'll remind you of the favor every time they want you to do something for them.

This happens a lot in friendships and even in workplace relationships. Often when you turn them down, they'll counter by saying, "you owe me." A boss who gives you a promotion can use that to get you to come in during the weekend. A colleague who covered for you once when you had to attend to a personal matter can use it to manipulate you into helping her with her projects.

Pity is also a common emotion that manipulators can use to get things from you. They'll tell you stories that inspire pity towards them, then when they are done; they'll ask you to do something to alleviate their "pain."

For example, a colleague could come to you and lament about how much workload he has been handling lately, and how unbearable it has become for him. You'll feel like you have to say something, and you'll go ahead and express empathy towards them. Once they see that you have a sense of compassion and kindness, they'll keep tugging at those strings, until they get you to ask, "How can I help?"

If you don't readily offer to help, they'll strongly imply that they could use someone's help without asking directly. If this doesn't work, they'll just go ahead and ask you point-blank. Experienced manipulators know that if you volunteer to help on your own, they can exploit you a lot more than if they had to ask you to help. To them, the offer to help is a blank check that they can fill however they like.

We also tend to have a fear of being alone, and manipulators can take advantage of that as well. Manipulators can seek out people who have low self-esteem, and feel like they don't have that many options when it comes to finding romantic partners or friends. In this case, manipulators will mistreat their victims, but then keep the victims from defending themselves by playing on their fear of loneliness. They'll say things like "I'm the only one that can love you" and "No one else would want you." When manipulators keep reminding us of our fear of loneliness, it can escalate to the point that it becomes crippling.

Manipulators can also use shame to get us to do what they want. Shame is a particularly strong emotion, and it can take many forms. Shame is an agonizing feeling that results from a sense of incorrectness, or inferiority. People will do anything to avoid shame, and manipulators often count on that fact.

Shame is highly subjective, which means that manipulators can get us to be ashamed of things that we don't originally consider to be shameful. They'll convince you to be ashamed of things that you've always been okay with. They'll try to make you feel ashamed for failing to meet their expectations. When they manage to sow the seed of shame in you, they gain the power to control you.

Manipulators can also exploit people's sense of vanity. They'll observe people and figure out what things they are vain about; then they'll use vainglory against them.

Manipulators also exploit other's sense of hope. Hope can be a strong emotion, especially in people who are experiencing major challenges. When a manipulator has you under his control, and you want to break free, he will introduce a glimmer of hope to indicate to you that things could get better, just to get you to stay.

If he is abusive, he could claim that he is "working on it," so you stick around, hoping that he will better himself. If there is something specific that you are hoping to get out of the relationship, he will keep promising to deliver on it, but then, he'll come up with new excuses to push the deadline further.

# Lying

Lying is a manipulation technique on its own, but it's also an essential part of every other manipulation technique out there. All forms of manipulation involve some level of deception. Manipulators, predators, and abusers tend to be better liars than the average person; in fact, many of them are pathological liars.

The worst kinds of manipulators not only lie to others, but they also lie to themselves. This is known as self-deception. Some people tend to rationalize the evil they do to the extent that they start believing that it's good, or it's in the best interest of the people they are manipulating or deceiving.

Lying is said to be the ultimate manipulation tactic because, as we've mentioned, it's a part of every other technique. Manipulators learn to lie as a matter of habit. Sometimes, they lie even when it's purposeless (it's their way of sharpening their deception skills).

Lying serves many different purposes for manipulators. In many cases, it gives them some sort of advantage over the people they are manipulating. The way they see it, it's never in their best interest  for you to get to know them, because that would increase your chances of figuring out what they are up to, so, most of the time, they'll misrepresent themselves to you, even if it doesn't seem to be objectively necessary.

This means that lying is often the first sign that you are dealing with a manipulator. So, whether you are starting a new relationship, or you are getting acquainted with a new colleague or friend, if you catch them on a lie, no matter how small it is, you should know that it could be indicative of something much larger; perhaps they are manipulators looking to win your trust before revealing their true intentions.

Everyone tends to lie on occasion. Ordinary people lie because they are trying to avoid confrontation with others (if you think telling someone the truth will lead to them reacting explosively, you might decide it's in your own best interest to lie). People also lie to avoid hurting others (you wouldn't tell your spouse or friend that they don't look good when they have put some work into making a fashion statement). Some people also lie for economic or financial expediency (you would lie on your resume to increase your chances of getting a decent job).

The fact is that we are all socially conditioned to lie to some extent, even though we believe in the principle that we should always tell the truth. The kinds of lies that everyone tells are called "white lies." They don't usually hurt anyone, and sometimes, they actually help people. However, when manipulative people lie, it's usually to the extent that is beyond what can be accepted as social conditioning.

For manipulators, lying is about control. When they lie, it makes it possible for them to control others. They often have low self-esteem, or they experience fear-based thoughts, so they believe that the only way to get people to do what they want is through deception. Take the example of people who lie to get others to fall in love with them. If they were honest, they'd probably still get others to care about them and fall in love with them, but they deliberately choose deception because they don't like who they are, so they feel compelled to misrepresent themselves.

Lying can be defined in several different ways. The most basic definition of lying is; making a statement that one knows to be false, with the express intention of deceiving or manipulating a person for personal gain. However, lying entails much more than just deceptive statements.

You can lie by intentionally giving false impressions about someone or something. You can lie by creating a circumstance which gives a false impression for your own gain. You can also lie by deceiving yourself, and then imposing the erroneous believes that you have about yourself on others. You can lie by telling certain facts and hiding other "redemptive" facts about a person or a thing. Manipulators are aware of all these forms of lying, and they use them every day on the people they target.

Misinformation is one of the most common lying techniques that manipulators like to use. Misinformation involves the creation and perpetuation of false stories, and the point is to either deceive or to manipulate the persons being targeted.

Such stories end up being believable for 2 reasons. The first is that they are pathologically conceived (they are created in such an expertly fashion, that the person hearing them has no reason to doubt them). The second is that the level of importance of the core idea is exaggerated, but other than that, the story is mostly factual.

Misinformation is similar to disinformation with one key difference: while misinformation introduces new information to create new beliefs in a person, disinformation introduces new beliefs to challenge current ones by confusing the person.

Misinformation works in a number of ways. First, the person who is the target of the misinformation campaign may believe the story he is being told. Secondly, the person may be confused by the story, to the point he starts to doubt his convictions (so the misinformation works because it diverts attention from real issues). Third, misinformation can cause argument, or it can create dissent (this also serves to distract from real issues).

Finally, misinformation may introduce deliberate ambiguity in a situation (this way, the manipulator using it can later claim that you misunderstood him).

Derailment is also a common lying technique that's used by manipulators. Instead of the person providing a clear and direct response to your line of questioning, he will change the subject to something that is bound to rile you up, so that you waste time engaging in a pointless debate, and you end up forgetting about your questions.

Finally, manipulators like to use lies of omission against the people they manipulate. Lies of omission are very pervasive, and they are in fact more common than direct lies (lies of commission).

Manipulators love these kinds of lies. They can use them to turn your friends and family against you and to create animosity between you and your mutual acquaintances. They can also make certain insinuations about themselves, and then let you believe things about them which they know aren't true.

For manipulators, lying is also a way of avoiding accountability for their actions and refusing to change. If you notice that someone has a certain vice and you want to help him change, but he denies having the vice, he could be a manipulator.

## Guilt Tripping

Guilt-tripping is a manipulation tactic that involves making someone feel guilty about something, with the aim of incentivizing them to behave, feel, or act in a way that benefits the manipulator, often to the detriment of the person being guilt-tripped.

In many cases, the person laying the guilt-trip (the manipulator) often wants his or her target to either apologize for certain actions or to offer them something to assuage their guilt. Guilt-tripping works by making the target feel like they won't be forgiven unless they do something that the manipulator wants.

When a manipulator wants to guilt trip you to get you to apologize for something that happened to them (whether or not it was your fault), they'll often start by trying to get you to admit to some form of wrongdoing. They know that the moment you admit to doing something wrong, they gain the power to make certain demands from you.

Often, they won't come right out and accuse you of something. Instead, they'll build towards it by asking you leading questions. They know that if they use a direct approach, it could end up as some kind of argument, and they won't be able to induce guilt if you are angry.

For example, if you come home late, and they want you to feel guilty about it, they won't state that outright. They may start by asking where you were, and why you didn't pick up the phone when they called. They'll often try to entrap you into lying so that they can catch you on the lie and pile on to your guilt.

For instance, the person guilting you for coming home late will ask things like "Were you at work?" even though they called the office and weren't able to reach you there either (if you take the bait and lie, you now have 2 things to be guilty about instead of just one).

Manipulative people tend to be very flexible in the way they guilt-trip others. If the thing they are trying to accuse you of doesn't stick, they can often pivot and make it about something else entirely.

After accusing you of something and getting you to admit it, the person laying the guilt trip will often bring up some of your other past "transgressions" with the aim of compounding your mistakes and establishing a pattern of behavior. This is especially common if the initial mistake isn't such a big deal. Here, they may play the victim and list all the cases where they have felt victimized by you.

If they are accusing you of coming home late, they may point out all the times you have done the same thing. They'll also remind you of something bad you did, which they let go (this helps to show how saintly they are, and it keeps you from bringing up any counter-arguments because you would come across as ungrateful).

After laying out your transgressions in detail, it's time for them to play with your feelings. Here, they'll say something like, "How can you claim you love me, and then you do this to me?" or "Don't I matter to you?" To multiply your guilt, they'll then bring up some of the great things that they have done for you. When they list their saintly qualities, those qualities will be juxtaposed with your evil ones, and it will be plain to see that you've been bad to them when they were good to you. That they've given you their trust and you have abused it.

After that, it will be your turn to speak, but they won't let you. They know that their argument isn't entirely logical, and if they give you the stage, you could explain how each accusation wasn't entirely your fault, so they won't let you put out a coherent thought. They'll deflect all your attempts to explain yourself, or to turn the situation around and make it their fault. They'll try to get you angry because if you lose your temper, it only plays further into their hands.

To elicit guilt in you, the manipulator will amp up their emotions and make things really uncomfortable if they notice that an admission of guilt isn't coming, or that you are trying to stay calm and rational. They'll express exaggerated negative emotions. They may start crying (more likely to happen with women) or yelling (more likely to happen with men). You may become so desperate to calm the other person down; you may decide it's no longer worth it to stand your ground. So, you'll apologize.

When manipulators are guilt-tripping you in order to get something from you, they'll follow pretty much the same process, but towards the end, they'll focus more on playing with your feelings than on expressing negative emotions.

In this case, they'll start by highlighting the good things that they have done for you lately. Depending on what they are asking for, they might also guilt you by highlighting the good things they might be able to do once you give them what they want.

Even though it's not their main area of focus this time around, negative emotions may still come into play when someone wants something from you. In fact, manipulators like to use their targets' negative emotions to their benefit. Part of the reason guilt-tripping works is that the feeling of guilt is closely associated with negative emotions like sadness, anger, shame, and pity. Manipulators can get you to give them something by making you ashamed of how you've treated them, by making you angry or pitiful about how other people treated them, or by making you sad about the state of affairs they find themselves in.

Guilt-tripping also works because manipulators equate the things that they want out of you with the love that you have for them. They create the impression that your compliance with their demands is proportional to the love you have for them, or the happiness you wish for them to experience.

If you turn down a manipulative person after a guilt trip, that wouldn't be the end of it. They'll find other reasons to make you feel guilty again, and they'll keep piling on until you do as they wish.

## Silent Treatment

The silent treatment may seem like a normal part of any relationship, but it's a manipulation technique. Most of us have been on either the giving or receiving end of the silent treatment at some point in our lives, so it may not seem like something that's out of the ordinary.

You may have stayed silent after someone did something to set you off because you were trying to refrain from saying something drastic that could irrevocably ruin your relationship. If you are like most people, you broke the silence after the initial annoyance was over, and you were able to resolve whatever issues you had with the other person (whether it was a partner, a friend, and family member or a colleague).

The silent treatment may also be good for your mental health if you use it after a breakup (when you avoid getting in touch with your ex until you feel emotionally stable again).

However, manipulative people don't use it in either of those ways. They use the silent treatment as a weapon against those they wish to manipulate.

As a manipulation technique, the silent treatment involves refusing to speak to a person (who you normally talk to on a regular basis) for a prolonged period of time. It involves being unresponsive when they address you or acting as if they don't exist.

The silent treatment is considered by psychologists to be a form of emotional abuse. When you use it against someone, what you are doing is you are withholding from them, and emotional withholding can be rather punishing. In a personal relationship, your partner may use it to make you feel like an outsider. In professional relationships, the person may refuse to give you valuable information that could make it impossible for you to perform some of your job functions. In extreme cases, the person may make you feel ostracized from your social circle. If you have mutual friends, he or she may host an event, invite all your friends, and leave you out of the guest list.

So, what does the silent treatment accomplish? Well, ignoring someone is a way of controlling them. When you are in a relationship with someone, you get close to them, and you may even be codependent in some ways. If they start ignoring you and giving you the silent treatment, then they have you over a barrel, because you are at a point in your life where you need their input just to function normally. If it's your spouse, you probably have to make joint decisions with them, so if they don't talk to you, you'll have to postpone all your decisions.

If the person wants something from you, and he or she makes it clear that the only way he or she would talk to you is if you comply with their request, you may decide that it's no longer worth it to stand your ground.

A manipulative person may also use the silent treatment to avoid doing their jobs or taking responsibility for their actions. At work, a colleague may find fault in you and decide to give you the silent treatment when a joint project is almost due;

since he or she isn't talking to you, it would be impossible to get their input, so you would have to do everything on your own.

If you call out a partner for doing something wrong, he or she might give you the silent treatment instead of owning up and apologizing, and you might be forced to let things go just to keep the peace.

Manipulators who use the silent treatment are mostly those who have difficulties communicating (they never learned to play well with others) and they are used to getting their way. In childhood, they might have been given a lot of attention by their parents (to an unhealthy extent), so they expect people attend to their emotional needs even if they don't do a good job of expressing them.

People who like to take up the victim role may use the silent treatment because they are genuinely afraid of confrontation. They go silent because they want their partner to think of them as the victims in whatever conflict they are having.

People also tend to use the silent treatment because they want their partners to be afraid of losing them. If they know that their partner is insecure (e.g., if he or she is afraid of being alone), they may use the silent treatment to indicate to the partner that the assertions they are making could cause a rift which in turn could lead to a breakup. They expect the other person to back down out of fear that the relationship could end.

In extreme cases, the silent treatment could be damaging to a person's mental health. As social beings, our mental health depends on how well we get along with others in social contexts, so when someone ignores us or ostracizes us, it could have serious implications for use. Studies show that people who are emotionally abused are more likely to experience stress-related disorders than the rest of the population (this is especially true among women). In cases where the person is repeatedly exposed to the silent treatment, the mental health implications are even much worse.

Of all types of manipulators, narcissists are the ones who are most likely to use silent treatment against their targets or victims. That's because they lack empathy, and they generally believe that they are superior to others: When a narcissist gives you the silent treatment, he or she is making the point that interacting with him, or her is a privilege for you, one that he can take away if he wishes to, unless you do what he wants. Narcissists may also give you the silent treatment because they are afraid that if they engage with you in a mature conversation, you may come off looking smarter than them.

## Weakness

Manipulators will often feign weakness as a way of making you feel more responsible for them so that you end up attending to their needs instead of taking care of yourself. Feigning weakness is sometimes referred to as "playing the victim." It may seem counter-intuitive, but portraying oneself as weak is one of the most effective ways to control others.

If you control someone by trying to show that you are strong and you can force them to comply with your needs, they may do what you want, but it won't be out of their own will (so they'll do the bare minimum. However, if you pretend to be weak, and you manipulate the person into feeling that they are responsible for helping you, they'll offer to help out of their own will, meaning they'll put in their best effort.

You can tell that someone is using weakness as a manipulation technique against you if they don't seem to take responsibility for themselves, and they keep implying that you should. If they cause a problem, they'll portray themselves as either victims or martyrs, and they'll make it clear that it's beyond their means to fix the problem.

Such manipulators will try to make it seem that they are at the mercy of everything and everyone in their environment. When they come into your life for the first time, they may show that they have drive and ambition, but once they are in, they'll become "frozen."

They'll come up with excuses for not making any progress in their lives; usually, they'll be things that portray them as powerless. Such manipulators have an uncanny ability to generate a quick laundry list of excuses to explain why they can't be productive; they'll give you as many excuses as possible until they stumble upon one that sticks. If you ask them to come up with a plan to get out of the situation they are in, they'll then give you excuses why they can't come up with a plan.

When you try to hold such people accountable, they may resort to using other manipulation techniques (such as guilt-tripping) to get you off their backs. Some may be lazy people who want to leach off you for as long as they can. This mostly works with people who are related to you because there is a strong sense of obligation to help in such cases.

Manipulators who use weakness as a technique often spend a lot of time feeling sorry for themselves. They want to present themselves as pitiable, so given the opportunity, they'll portray themselves as defenseless children who need to be attended to all the time. When they have a tough day, they'll talk about it like it's the most torturous human experience in history. They'll also want to seem immature, especially around people who feel that they have no choice but to offer their help.

Manipulators also use weakness by negatively comparing themselves to others. They often point out the advantages that others have over them, and they always conclude that those advantages are unfair. If someone got a job promotion over them, they'd claim that it was because of favoritism. They'll make it sound as though external circumstances are conspiring in favor of other people and against them.

These people also tend to hold on to grudges, especially if they serve their purposes. To them, grudges are weapons that they can use to blame others for their own failure, with the intention of making others feel guilt and a sense of obligation towards them. The grudges they hold often sound misgiven when stated out loud.

For example, a partner may claim that the reason he doesn't have a job is that you failed to remind him about his interview appointment 3 years ago. He will bring up old events and cite them as the reasons for his failure, even when any objective person would have moved past those events.

People can feign weakness, not just to manipulate you, but also to abuse you. When a person is abusive, they may pretend to be the weaker ones in the relationship so that people don't think of them as the aggressors.

When in public, they may feign all the signs of weakness so that anyone looking at you as a couple immediately jumps to the conclusion that he or she doesn't have what it takes to abuse somebody. It can be incredibly frustrating if you know you are the real victim, but the other person has the sympathy of everyone in your social circle.

Manipulators can also portray weakness as a way of justifying their cruelty, at least to themselves. Psychologists use transactional analysis as a method of explaining most relationship dynamics. In transactional analysis, there is a theory that when people experience cognitive dissonance due to their actions, they tend to alter their behavior to match what they believe about themselves. Manipulative people like to believe that they are good people even though their brains tell them that they aren't, so they'll play the part of a weaker person as a way to find a balance between the evil they do, and the way they want to perceive themselves.

Weakness is commonly used by manipulative people with substance abuse problems to get other people to take care of them. Alcoholics and drug users understand that their problems are technically illnesses, and some of them can take advantage of that fact to get people to take responsibility for them. They may use weakness to guilt family members and friends, and to excuse some of their worst impulses.

Weakness is the ultimate attention seeking manipulation technique. People who use it essentially tell others that "I can't do anything for myself without your help." Manipulators who use it tend to seek out victims who are patient and compassionate.

## Dirty Looks

Dirty looks are those scornful glances that people give to each other to indicate they don't approve. Dirty looks may seem ultimately harmless at face value, but they have a serious emotional toll of the people who are on the receiving end of such gestures. That explains why men get into confrontations and bar fights over dirty looks, and why women turn into mortal enemies over the same. Dirty looks are, in fact, a very big deal, and manipulators are aware of this fact.

You may wonder, why is it so disconcerting when someone shoots you a dirty look? Well, the reason is quite simple. We are all very self-conscious. Even those among us with high self-esteem still worry about what others think of us. When you walk into a room, you worry about what people think of your outfit, your general demeanor, or even your presence in the room.

As a way to cope with self-consciousness, we tell ourselves that people have positive thoughts about us. However, when someone shoots you a dirty look, that illusion is shattered, and worse, in many cases, you are left with no idea of what you did wrong. As a result, the self-consciousness comes back, and this times, it's multiplied. If you are an aggressive person (like the macho guys at the bar), you may snap and demand an explanation from the guy who shot you the look.

Manipulators use dirty looks in different ways, and to different ends. For example, there are studies that show that women in the workplace can shake each other's confidence using a specific kind of dirty look. The manipulator, in this case, would look the target up and down, and then put on a sneer, as though to indicate contempt.

With this look alone, the target may start thinking that there is something wrong with her appearance or her presentation, and this could affect the way she conducts herself for the rest of the day. If this is done repeatedly, every day, the target may start feeling a sense of inferiority, and that could affect her job performance. If those two women are on the same career path, the manipulative one may be able to gain an advantage over her target, just with dirty looks!

As a manipulation technique, dirty looks work on women more than on men. In many surveys, women had indicated that they are more likely to feel pressure to buy new clothes or to wear more make-up if other women gave them a dirty look, even when those women were their close friends, and they knew for a fact that the dirty looks had nothing to do with their appearance.

People in marketing and advertising are aware of this fact, and they sometimes use dirty looks to get women to purchase certain products. Some fashion stores will employ perfect-looking, well-dressed women to work on their sales teams, and they'll instruct them to give judgmental looks to the women who walk into the store in order to increase their chances of making a purchase.

In abusive relationships, dirty looks can be used to control victims in a public setting. There are different kinds of dirty looks, and people who have been in a relationship for long tend to gain an understanding of what their partner's dirty looks mean. If your controlling partner is across the room, and he shoots you a certain look, you might be able to tell if he is unhappy with you interacting with someone, if he is giving you the look because of an unresolved argument you had earlier, or if he is tired of being there and he wants the both of you to leave.

Manipulators and abusive partners work hard to maintain all appearances of normalcy when you are in public. Since they can't yell at you or physically control you while everyone is looking, they'll shoot you dirty looks to get you to do what they want. They'll try to do it in a subtle way so that no one else notices.

Dirty looks can also be used to manipulate people, even if they are total strangers. Some "pick up artists" give the women they are targeting dirty looks with the aim of making them self-conscious and lowering their self-worth. The idea is that when they approach those women latter, the women will feel like they have something to prove, and as a result, they may comply with the man's sexual advances.

## Voice Changes and Word Choices

Words are extremely powerful manipulation tools, and the way we say them makes them even more potent. Word choice and voice changes are used in almost every form of manipulation that we have discussed thus far in the book. With manipulators, everything they say is carefully calculated to advance certain agendas that they have. They also use different pitches to indicate sarcasm, mockery, heightened negative emotions, etc. whenever they need to.

Emotional manipulation goes hand in hand with verbal communication. People use language in a way that benefits them and harms others all the time. Language can be used to control others or to convince them to act against their own best interests. Words can damage a person's self-esteem, ruin a person's reputation, or even destroy their identity.

Manipulators use carefully chosen words to distort facts. All manipulators are, to some extent, experts in twisting the truth to serve their own interests. Manipulators would use carefully chosen words to avoid taking responsibility for certain things or even to blame you for what has gone wrong. When they tell stories about you, they'll use their words to portray themselves as heroes and you as the villain.

Manipulators also use "intellectual harassment" to emotionally manipulate their victims. Intellectual harassment refers to a technique where the manipulator would initiate lots of arguments with you get you to engage with them in verbal contests that are not constructive. They may try to use facts and figures to win arguments over you, or to get you to think that they are way smarter than you are.

You could be talking about an issue in your relationship, and suggesting a solution to it, but then they counter with some "scientific study" they read about, or they may even try to focus on your grammar instead of talking about the issue at hand.

They may use convoluted reasoning to try to make a point that is clearly unnecessary, with the aim of making your whole discussion about something else entirely. The purpose of intellectual harassment is to convince you to see things their way, and if that doesn't work, they'll settle for you getting emotionally exhausted to the point that you can no longer argue with them.

Manipulators also tend to repeat their targets' names in conversations as a way of manipulating them. When someone says your name, you pay attention to them, and if they are trying to convince you of something, it makes you engage with them on a personal level, and it increases the chances of you agreeing to comply with your request.

However, in arguments, especially those that occur in public, the manipulator may repeat your name, often in an exaggerated tone, to throw you off balance, or to make other people pay attention. In such cases, the aim might be to embarrass you or to put you on the spot. Because people are watching, and they keep hearing your name, you might feel awkward or intimidated, and you are likely to give in to what the other person wants, just to get people's eyes away from you.

Manipulative people also use irony and dark humor to humiliate their victims in public. They may make ironic comments about a person's appearance or any other personal qualities. The aim here is to belittle the victim, to make him or her an object of public mockery, and to destroy his or her self-esteem.

The use of irony is deliberate because it offers the manipulator a cop-out in case they are confronted. For example, if the victim decides to assert herself and tell off the manipulator, he might say that he was just joking and that the victim should get a sense of humor. This can be doubly embarrassing for the victim.

People who use irony against others are usually trying to make themselves seem superior to the other person as if they are above it all, when deep inside, they are trying to conceal negative emotions like jealousy or insecurity.

Another way manipulators use words to manipulate their victims is by letting them go first in conversations. In most arguments, the person who goes last has an inherent advantage over the one who goes first, because he gets more control over how the argument will end. Some controlling people will let you say what you want to say.

When you are done, they'll speak after you, counter all the points you have made, make their own points, conclude in their favor, say the debate is over, and that it was fair because everyone got to share their feelings.

Other controlling people will let you go first because they want to hear all your good points so that they can come up with strategies to decimate them. In such cases, they may not even bother to come up with their own arguments. They'll just point out the shortcomings in yours and make fun of you.

Some manipulator may verbally manipulate you by portraying you as irrational, and claiming that it's impossible to talk to you. They can even bait you into acting irrationally so they can appear to be the level headed ones. When you argue with someone, and you raise your voice slightly, they could latch onto that and ask you to stop screaming and being emotional.

This can turn into a vicious circle; when someone asks you to calm down, you naturally feel irritated with their patronizing attitude, and so instead of calming down, you do the exact opposite. Before you know it, you find that you've forgotten the points you were trying to make, and you are now arguing about your emotions. This way, the manipulative person keeps you from addressing the topic at hand.

## Love Smothering

It's said that too much of anything poison. When love is expressed excessively, oftentimes, it ceases to be love, and it becomes manipulation. Love smothering is the manipulation technique that involves comical displays of affection which end up making the recipient uncomfortable.

Love smothering stems from a need to control the other person because the manipulator is afraid that he or she might leave. some psychologists also refer to it as "love bombing" (although the term love bombing is more commonly used to refer to love smothering during the period when the recipient still thinks it's charming, before he or she realizes that the other person is just being clingy and that this poses a real problem for the relationship).

Love smothering often starts out feeling good. The two people get into a relationship, and everything seems normal. The manipulator will perform grand gestures to show his or her affection for the target, and the target may think of these gestures as excessive, but also endearing and romantic.

The gestures will make the relationship feel special; they may include love notes being left around the house, compliments that are deeply flattering, or flowers being delivered to the target's place of work. These gestures seem nice at first, but when they persist and escalate, they start affecting the target's ability to function normally.

Love mothering is different from real-love for many reasons. First of all, smothering isn't done out of real affection for the other person. It's done out of selfishness. The person doing the smothering isn't considering how the other one feels, he is just motivated by his own insecurities, and he is seeking to convince the other person to stay.

Smothering serves to control the target. The manipulative person knows full well that you enjoy spending time with your family and your friends, but he or she would want to take up all your time and be part of every activity that you do.

The manipulator would want you to choose him over everyone else, even if it seems completely irrational. He could feel threatened by everyone in your life, even if it's your own family members or your children. He will want to know who you are with at all times, what you are doing, where you are going, what's in your handbag, who you were just talking to on the phone, who sent that text that just made you smile etc.; it just gets more irrational by the minute.

Manipulators use love smothering by consistently seeking attention and validation from you. You'll find that they are constantly asking you to reassure them, to tell them how much you love them. They'll want to know if you love them more than other people, even where the comparison is unwarranted. They'll ask things like "Do you love me more than you love your mother?" When you give them attention, it makes them feel important, as if they are at the center of your universe.

Smothering is often characterized by high levels of impatience and inflexibility. If manipulators don't get the attention they want or if you are busy and don't spend time with them, they become irritated, angry, highly agitated, and they get rather irrational. Even if you say something came up at work, they won't ever listen to reason. If you are trying to deal with something and you ask them to be patient, they'll won't give you any light of day. They'll become clingy.

As a result of all these, such manipulator end up being overwhelming and suffocating. Breaking up with them can be quite dangerous as well. People who use love smothering tend to be narcissists or even psychopaths, and when you reject them (as they've always feared), they'll feel the need to either do something crazy to win you back, or they'll try to do something harmful to punish you for hurting them.

After breaking up, a smothering person might stalk you, try to get to you through friends and mutual acquaintances, or even get into altercations with the people you go out with.

# Chapter 5: How to Recognize Mind and Emotional Control, and Deception

As we have already mentioned in the book, many people end up under the control of manipulators because they fail to recognize the earliest signs that the person they are dealing with is controlling. Men and women alike find themselves in toxic relationships without any idea of how they got into them in the first place.

There is one main reason why so many people end up falling into the traps set for them by controlling people; they buy into the stereotypes of what controlling, or manipulative person are like, and they give normal-looking people a pass as a result.

When you think of a controlling person, it might be easy for you to form a mental picture of what that person might look like. It's always a "crazy" psychopathic person, like the villains we see in movies. That is a problem because it prevents us from considering the possibility that the mild-mannered people we encounter every day could also turn out to be controlling and malicious.

When someone approaches you with charisma, and he seems normal by all appearances, it might be difficult to even conceive of the possibility that he is a bad person, but the fact is that you are more likely to be manipulated by the "boy next door" or "girl next door" type, than to be targeted by someone who shows the stereotypical signs of psychopathy.

In this chapter, let's look at how you can recognize the signs of mental and emotional control; especially those that are most likely to fly below your radar.

People who try to control others will start out by isolating them from their family and friends. It always starts in a very subtle way, and in most cases, you might not even realize that there is a problem with what the manipulator is doing.

When the manipulator starts dating you, he might start by complaining about some of your friends and family. He might complain about how often you talk to your siblings on the phone, claiming that you should give more attention to the relationship instead. He might also point out that he doesn't like some of your friends, claiming that they are a bad influence on you, and he might try to convince you to stop hanging out with them.

Once you have gotten close enough for you to feel invested in the relationship, he might try to make you choose between hanging out with him and hanging out with your friends. You might decide to do as he says because you feel like it's a small concession that you are making, but that just leads you into a trap.

We all have support systems in our lives; people who care about us, and they would try to stand up for us when they see that someone is taking advantage of us. The controlling person will try to weaken your support systems and isolate you so that when he tries to control you, there aren't any objective observers to warn you or stand up for you.

So, if you notice that the new guy in your life is trying to drive a wedge between you and your friends and family, or that he is trying to tell you who you can or can't be friends with, that should indicate to you that he is controlling.

Manipulative and controlling people tend to be chronically critical of their targets. If you notice that the new person in your life is highly critical, even of the small things you do, you could be dealing with someone who has the intention of controlling you.

Just like isolation, criticism is something that starts on a small scale early in a relationship, and it grows over time as the manipulative person becomes more emboldened.

In many cases, when you notice that someone is critical of you early in the relationship, you might try to convince yourself that the criticism is somehow warranted, or you might even give the person points for being bold and open about how he feels. You might think that he just wants you to be a better person, or you might rationalize the criticism by convincing yourself that you could just make those small changes to make them happy.

The problem is that when a person is criticizing the things that are part of who you are when the relationship is still new, you can be certain that this is going to be a constant dynamic for the duration of that relationship.

Try to look at it through the long lenses. If you have only known him for a week or two and in that time, he has asked you to change the way you dress, the décor of your apartment, or your style of cooking, then how much is he going to ask you to change if he was to be a part of your life for the next 2 years? What about after you've been married for 15 years?

Our personalities are the totality of the small things we do every day. So, if you change one or two things about yourself every week because a critical person asked you to do it, in a few years, he would have managed to change your personality completely; and we can guarantee that it won't be for the better.

People who are critical also tend to make you doubt yourself, and this will slowly chip away at your self-esteem over time. If you internalize their criticism, it will get to a point where you start looking for their approval in everything that you do; so, you will be doing whatever they ask you to because you want to feel loved, accepted and validated. In other words, they would have gained full control over you without you realizing it.

So, no matter what kind of relationship it is, you should treat all forms of criticism with suspicion. If a new boyfriend seems to criticize everything you do; he is a controlling person, and you should get away from him as soon as you can.

If your boss or college criticizes everything you do, try to objectively assess the merit of each critical comment he makes, and figure out whether or not its constructive criticism; at work, constructive criticism comes with suggestions on how you can do better, but when manipulators criticize you, they do it to belittle you and make you feel like you are not up to the task.

Another clear sign that you are dealing with a controlling person is that they'll try to leverage their affection towards you by making it conditional on certain things. The love, affection, attraction, or acceptance that you get from them will be contingent on something else.

It could be that they want you to change something about yourself for them to give you affection, or it could be that they want you to give them something specific in return for that affection.

At times this can manifest itself fairly early in the relationship, but it's more likely to occur in relationships that are already established; it's much easier to leverage someone when they already feel invested in a relationship.

For example, a man could tell a woman he has been dating for a while that he won't be intimate with her unless she loses a few pounds. A woman could tell a man that she wouldn't get engaged to him unless he started making more money at his job. There are less blatant examples of how this may play out, but the underlying assertion is the same; "Unless you change, I won't love you as much." If the person you are seeing makes any assertion that has this implication, he or she is controlling, and you should get out of that relationship before it's too late.

You can also recognize mind or emotional control by assessing a person's tendencies to use veiled threats against you or against other people.

Threats don't necessarily have to include a promise physical violence, or even to suggest adverse negative consequences for you. Threats, in this context, refer to any insinuations that a person might leave you, cut off certain "privileges" that they are offering you, or even harm themselves if you do or don't act in certain ways.

If early in the relationship, you find yourself taking certain actions, not because you want to, but because you are concerned about what the other person might think or feel, or how he or she might react, then that person could be manipulating you, and it's only going to get worse moving forward.

At the beginning of the relationship, the person may insinuate that they won't hang out with you unless you take them to fancy restaurants or buy them certain gifts to show your affection. A few years down the line, you might feel like you are trapped in the relationships because the person insinuates that if you break up with them, they'll commit suicide, or they'll make false public accusations against you, or they'll keep you from seeing your children.

Once you notice that someone likes to make threats to control you, no matter how small or well veiled those threats are, you should take the situation very seriously. When small threats work, manipulators get emboldened, and they start issuing bigger threats.

You should also pay attention to people's tendencies to use guilt as a weapon against others because guilt is particularly effective when it comes to controlling people. When someone uses guilt against you, they are making your own emotions work in their favor.

You might be able to notice this tendency early in a relationship; if the person capitalizes on every little transgression you make to get the maximum utility out of it, then you can be certain that they'll be guilt-tripping you for the rest of your relationships. If you are five minutes late to a date, and the person makes you feel like you've betrayed them in some way and you need to atone for it, then you can be sure that they are the kind of people who will keep a score of every little thing you do and use it to make you feel bad about yourself.

If you start going out with someone who makes you apologize for every little thing that most people would just let go, then this can also be a sign that they'll be using guilt to manipulate you for years to come.

You can also recognize a controlling person by how much they like to keep score whenever they do you a favor. Now, reciprocity is a vital component in any kind of relationship; the other person will do certain favors for you, and you will feel the need to do different favors for them in return; that is just natural.

However, if you notice that someone is particularly preoccupied with keeping scores, you can be certain that he or she is a controlling person. If you notice that they are taking note of every instance where they feel they deserve to get a favor in return for what they've done, where they think they are entitled to hold a grudge, or where they feel they deserve to be patted on the back, it could mean that you are dealing with someone who is hell-bent on getting the upper hand over you. In some cases, their aim might be to wear you down so that you admit that your life is nothing without their input.

You might also be able to notice if a person is controlling if you observe the way they come onto you at the beginning of the relationship. Controlling people tend to come on to their targets very strongly, and they tend to use exaggerated romantic gestures; this phenomenon is referred to as "love bombing."

The aim is to get the target to feel somehow beholden or indebted to the manipulative person. When someone does lots of great things for you at the beginning of the relationship, you will naturally feel like you owe them something, and you will be less likely to turn them down when they make certain requests from you.

In any blossoming relationship, there is a natural tendency for people to go a little out of their way to impress their love interests, but if someone does things that make you feel smothered, then it's a clear sign that they are controlling.

You can also identify a controlling person by the tactics that he or she uses to get information about you; if he or she uses underhanded techniques or methods that make you feel uncomfortable, then it's a clear sign that they are manipulative.

Controlling people feel like they have a right to know certain things about you. If a person acts like they are entitled to information that you would consider highly private, they are controlling. If they constantly snoop around and spy on you, it's because they feel it's their right to know where you are and what you do at all times.

Some of them may not even bother to snoop or spy; they'll try to make constant disclosures a requirement in your relationship. Every time you receive a call or text message, they'll ask you who it's from, and they may even do it under the guise of "open communication." They'll read your private messages, check your emails, and even keep track of your internet search history.

When you try to establish boundaries with them, they may play with your emotions by saying that they have trust issues because they have been cheated on before in past relationships. They may also play with your mind by telling you that if you have nothing to hide, then you wouldn't object to their snooping. No matter what justification the person may have, snooping and spying is a violation of your privacy; plain and simple.

When it comes to controlling people, the person who won't let you have any privacy in your life is perhaps the worst kind, because it means that they want to police the flow of information into your life – big brother style.

Controlling people also tend to be overly jealous, and they are likely to make lots of paranoid accusations in the early stages of your relationship. The reason most people miss this sign is that they sometimes think it's endearing.

When you are just getting started in a new relationship, it can be flattering to see that your new partner is jealous of potential rivals because it indicates that they are really into you; it can be easy to forget that it also means that they want to control who you associate with. As the relationship progresses, the person's level of possessiveness may get worse, and it could be accompanied by threats of physical violence.

When you internalize your partner's possessive nature, you will instinctively start watching out and avoiding interacting with other people, and that way the controlling person wins over you.

You can also tell if a person is controlling if he shows little or no respect for your personal time or boundaries. Manipulative people can sap away your strength just by insisting on being around you all the time. When you say you need some time to recharge or re-center yourself, they'll make you feel guilty or selfish.

We all need time alone once in a while. When you are alone, you can gather your thoughts, you can take stock of your life, and you can remind yourself what your real values are. This means that alone-time is crucial for maintaining your sense of self and your identity.

Controlling people will want to overwhelm you with their thoughts and ideas in order to change your world view, so they don't want you taking stock of your life. If a person you are dating won't come to a reasonable compromise on how much alone time you should get, you can be certain that they are controlling.

# Chapter 6: How to Defend Yourself against Mind and Emotional Manipulation

The first and most important thing that you need to do to defend yourself against mind and emotional control and manipulation is to accept the fact that the person you are dealing with is controlling and manipulative, and that's his or her nature.

The reason people stay with controlling individuals is that they operate under the misconception that such people can change. Many controlling and manipulative people tend to have dark personality traits such as narcissism, Machiavellianism, sadism, or psychopathy. That means that the need to control others is just part of who they are.

If you start dating someone (or associating with them in any other way) and you realize that they are controlling, don't delude yourself into thinking that you will be able to change them and make them less controlling. That is part of the manipulation; they'll put out signals that indicate to you that they might be open to change, but that only makes you feel more invested in the relationship, and it makes you susceptible to further manipulation and control.

Controlling people won't change on their own; the need to control others is primal, and it's not something that can be easily trained out of a person. So, once you see any of the signs of control that we discussed in the previous chapter, it's time for you to either sever your connection with the person, or if he or she is a permanent part of your life (like a family member that you can't completely avoid), you should start considering some of the defensive strategies that we will discuss in this chapter.

Once you have accepted that controlling people won't change on their own, it's time to come up with a strategy to deal with them. Towards that end, the first thing you need to do is ensure that you understand all your fundamental human rights, and make sure that the controlling person doesn't violate them.

You have every right to stand up and to defend your fundamental rights including: the right to be treated with respect; the right to set and pursue your own priorities; the right to express your own needs and feelings; the right to say "NO" to someone's request without feeling guilty about it; the right to have an opinion that differs from that of anyone and everyone else; the right to pursue a happy and healthy life; and the right to protect yourself from threats (including physical, mental, and emotional threats).

If someone infringes on any of these rights, you have a right to act. Controlling people will try to convince you otherwise. They'll tell you don't feel how you feel, or that they didn't mean something the way you interpreted it, but don't ever substitute your own objective judgment for someone else's; if you feel what the manipulator is doing is harmful to you, don't give them the chance to convince you otherwise, because no matter how smart you are, good manipulators will be able to talk you out of anything.

Think of the rights we have listed above as boundaries. Picture them as lines that separate you from everyone else; even the people you love. No one gets to cross those lines. Anyone who does is out to control you; we are not trying to get you to be paranoid, we are trying to get you to be vigilant. It's only by being vigilant that you will be able to see a controlling person come from a mile away, and you'll be able to strategize and to defend yourself.

You need to learn to tune into your real feelings in every situation that you find yourself in. The thing about controlling people is that they try their best to be subtle so that their manipulation techniques can fly under the radar. That means that if you are interacting with such people while you are on autopilot, it can be extremely difficult for you even to recognize the fact that they are trying to control you, so you won't be able to take defensive action.

Whenever anyone makes you have negative feelings, or they make you doubt your conviction about something, it's time to snap out of autopilot mode and tune in to the way you truly feel. Define the feeling. Is it guilt? Is it insecurity? Is it self-doubt? If you feel obligated to act a certain way, try to uncover the reason behind that sense of obligation: Are you afraid? Are you ashamed? Are you reciprocating? Unless you articulate your thoughts and feelings in such moments, you will be unable to tell when you are being manipulated.

Once you get the sense that you are being manipulated or someone is trying to control you, start scrutinizing everything they do. Manipulators work tirelessly to get you to fall into their trap. Every action they take will be tactfully selected to steer you one way or the other. The only way to avoid falling into their trap is by assuming that everything that they put on your path is a potential trap.

Since you know they are controlling, if they do something nice for you, try to identify the ulterior motive in their niceness. If they are mean to you, try to understand the objective behind their meanness. If you see they are trying to bait you into reacting in a specific way, avoid giving them the satisfaction.

People who are controlling like to pick soft targets, so if they see that the strategies they are deploying in the early stages of your association with them aren't working the way they are intended to, the manipulators might leave you alone and find someone else to target. If you don't seem to be malleable in any way, they'll won't want to waste their time on you.

You might also want to start keeping a record of all your interactions with manipulative people. This might seem excessive, but psychologists have long understood that writing things down (or keeping a journal) can help us make sense of the way we feel, and it can help put things into the right perspective.

There are several manipulation tactics that work because the victim stops believing in their own sense of right and wrong, and they stop trusting their own perceptions. When you write things down (preferably in an electronic journal), you can always refer back to it, and this will help ensure that you remain grounded in reality.

In cases of gas-lighting, manipulators can convince their victims that things didn't happen the way they remember. In cases of brainwashing, they can convince their victims that their feelings about certain past events aren't warranted, or that the memories they have are somehow warped. By keeping a journal, you'll have contemporaneous evidence of the things that happened and the way that you felt at the moment. This means that even if your memories fail you latter own, you will have a way of knowing the truth, and you'll, therefore, be less likely to let the controlling person convince you that you are wrong.

You can use either a physical journal or an electric one, but you have to make sure that the controlling person is unable to get his or her hands on it. Some people even use voice recording devices to keep records of their thoughts and emotions. Whatever method you choose, you should preserve and protect your own version of events because controlling people won't hesitate to rewrite your history.

You should also try to stay away from manipulative and controlling people. When you meet people for the first time, try to read their body language and their verbal cues, and try to figure out if they have ulterior motives. You can learn to read body language to help you detect when people are cunning or deceptive, but even without any training, you can learn to listen to your instincts about people and to trust those instincts.

Psychologists have established that the human mind can be able to accurately perceive potential threats within a few minutes of interacting with someone; try to differentiate between your instinctual reactions to a person and any prejudicial reactions or cognitive biases that you may have about certain demographics.

As we have mentioned several times in this book, manipulative people can come across as charming and charismatic, so, try to look past the superficial charm when you meet a person for the first time.

If the controlling person is a member of your family and you can't completely avoid them, try to keep your interactions to a bare minimum. Avoid spending time with them unless you have to, and avoid situations where you may find yourself alone with them.

If it's a college at work, you should try to steer away from them too, but make sure that your defensive action doesn't hurt your career. If the person is your boss, you might want to think about the long-term implications of working for a person like that. However, you can try to remain professional and to remind them to do the same whenever they cross the boundary and try to make things personal.

You can also deal with controlling people by calling them out and letting them know that you understand what they are doing. If you notice that someone is trying to manipulate you in a specific way, confront him, and tell him everything about his plan.

After reading this book, you understand the various tricks that manipulative and controlling people tend to use, so you may be able to identify what someone who is targeting you is trying to do. The next time they are up to their shenanigans, call them out on it. They may react in one of several ways. They may deny it and accuse you of being paranoid. They may fake outrage and try to guilt-trip you for making such serious accusation. They may react in anger since they know that their plan has been unraveled.

Whatever reaction the manipulator throws your way, you have to understand one thing; you are calling them out, not bargaining with them. So, if they try to convince you that you are wrong, just say something like "If you say so" and get away from them. Some of them will leave you and target someone else because they understand that you are too smart for their machinations.

However, others (especially the most malicious of the bunch) may try to retaliate against you with personal attacks, or they may switch strategies and try a different approach altogether. When they do this, call them out on that as well.

Sooner or later, even the more stubborn amongst them will start to realize that they aren't making any headway with you and they may give up. There are few who may take each instance of being called out as a challenge to step up their game; try to sever your connection with such people, or you can try calling them out in front of witnesses and warning them to stay away from you.

Again, as we've said, manipulative and controlling people tend to gravitate towards easy targets, so if you keep proving that you are no easy target, they'll recognize that they are wasting their effort.

You should also avoid getting emotionally attached to people who you suspect of being controlling. We acknowledge that this is easier said and done. Meeting new people isn't easy, so when you meet someone you think you might be compatible with, and you notice that they have certain traits that could indicate that they are controlling, it's still tempting to give them the benefit of the doubt, because deep within, we want to believe that people are good.

You might decide to indulge someone for a while before you fully understand his or her true nature, but as you do that, you become emotionally linked to them. you fall for their charming behavior, and before you gather enough evidence to prove to yourself that they are controlling conclusively, you would already be too emotionally invested in that relationships just to sever ties with them.

This can be compounded by the flawed thinking that we might be able to change people (which we discussed earlier). The best approach for you is to set your boundaries from day one before you become emotionally invested.

Even if you want to give the person the benefit of the doubt and to get to know them better, you should go into it while understanding your own rules, and don't let emotions cloud that understanding. Stay cordially civil whenever you interact with them (or anyone for that matter), and break with them as soon as you are sure that they are indeed as manipulative as you suspected.

So far, we have looked at how you can defend against mind and emotional control when you discover it early enough before you become too invested in a relationship. However, the fact is that even if you are vigilant, some people will fly under your radar, and they'll get close to you before you notice that they are manipulative. In other cases, you may not have a choice on whether or not such people are in your life; you may be able to choose your romantic partner, but you can't choose your family members, colleagues at work, or your casual acquaintances. So, how do you defend against control in such cases?

Well, you may be able to defend yourself by following this simple 3 step process:

## Know what you want

Manipulative people will seek to control you because they want something from you. They want something very specific from you, and they are manipulating or controlling you to increase their chances of getting that thing out of you. The problem is that if you are the kind of person who spends his or her time giving other people what they want, you will waste your whole life serving other people's interests, and you won't ever get what you really want out of life. So, no matter how long you have been under the influence of a manipulative person, this is how you have to start; by figuring out what is it that *you* want.

You have to do this as empirically and as systematically as possible. Take a notepad or some kind of writing material, and start evaluating the things that you consider to be your core values. Write down the things in your life that you believe are the most important to you. Is it your family? Your job? Your faith? Your academic pursuits? Certain hobbies you enjoy? A certain person you love? Be honest with yourself and create a list. First, write down whatever comes to mind. The first list will be in random order.

After you have put down all the things that you value, it's time for you to rank them according to how much you prioritize each one of them. List them, from what's most important to what's least important. Don't have any qualm or guilt about the way you rank your values (for example, if you feel your hobby is more important than your career, be honest with yourself in your rankings).

Once you have ranked your values, it's time for you to ask yourself why those values are important to you, and why each value is more important or less important relative to the other things in your list. Try to see if there are any things that you currently value, which may be on your list as a result of the machinations of a controlling person.

If there is a value that seems particularly important to you, or it seems to rank higher than it logically should, it could be up there because someone manipulative drilled it into you over a long period of time. If something that is logically important doesn't rank as highly as it should, it could be that a controlling person has been influencing you to think of it as unimportant.

You should also repeat the same exercise, and this time, instead of listing and ranking your values, you should list and rank your favorite ways to spend your free time. Start by listing all the activities that you believe you would like to do when you have the time. In this initial list, don't think practically; think imaginatively. If you had the time, and you had no constraints, no one to hold you back, what would you do?

You should then create a different list, not one of the activities you would lie to do, but one of all the activities that you remember doing during your personal time lately (all the time you spend outside work is technically person time). Rank those activities based on how much time you have spent on them in the past few months.

Now, compare those two lists and spot any differences. What would you like to do that you don't have the time to do? Why don't you have the time to do it? What takes up all your time? Look at the things that you often do, particularly those that take up most of your time. Why do you do those things? Do you truly enjoy doing them, or do you do them out of a sense of obligation? How much "me time" do you really get?

The reason why it's important to assess both your values and the way you spend your time is that someone may have taken over your life, and he may have installed his or her interests at the helm of all your lists.

A controlling person may have destroyed your real values, and he may have forced his values on you. A controlling person may be taking up all your time so that instead of doing what makes you happy, you are spending every free moment you have doing what makes him happy.

If you find yourself spending every evening in a sports bar with your boyfriend when you would rather be taking a dancing class, it means that he has taken control over your evenings and that his leisure activities are a bigger priority for you than your preferred leisure activities. If you find that most of your values are external rather than internal, it means that you care more about someone else's happiness more than your own.

Compare how things should be and how they are; if you find that your priorities are not your own, it's time to make a change.

## Stand your ground

Relationships (whether they are partnerships, marriages, friendships, or workplace relationships), are all about give-and-take. Controlling people and manipulators want to take more than they give or even more than you are willing to give. There is only one way to truly regain control if you are under the influence of a manipulative person, and that is to stand up to them.

Now that you know what you want, and you are able to identify areas in your life where you have compromised too much, and given control over to someone else, you'll have to confront the manipulative people in your life; there are no two ways about it. It's either you regain control, or you let them control you.

To stand up for yourself, you have to reinstate your real value and get rid of the values that have been imposed on you by manipulative people. If, when assessing your values, you realized that you don't have your priorities straight, it's time to let the people who take up your time know that from this point moving on, you will prioritize your own interests, and their interests will take the back seat.

You have to make it clear to yourself and to the people in your life that you have the same rights as they do, and you will no longer let them trample on those rights. Controlling people like to think that they are superior to the people they seek to control, so if you have one in your life right now, he or she is overdue for a reality check.

That's not to say that you should unload on such people, and release all your pent up anger onto them. you want to make it clear, and in the most logical of terms, that you will no longer be their personal doormat, that you won't be subservient to them, and that you do in fact, have the moral high ground in that situation.

Here are crucial tips that will help you stand up for yourself:

## Realize that no one else can invalidate you

The reason we are so afraid to stand up to controlling people is that we seek external validation. However, the whole concept of external validation is a fallacy. Sure, people can validate us; a boss can praise you in public, a spouse can tell others what a nice person you are, etc. when these people validate us, it only works if we choose to internalize that validation.

The same goes for invalidation. The only reason people have the power to invalidate us is we give them that power; we choose to internalize the invalidation. So, if you are afraid to stand up to someone because you think they'll invalidate you, for all intents and purposes, that's self-sabotage.

No matter what others say, the decision to perceive your thoughts, feelings, and actions as invalid only lies within you. This knowledge should empower you to stand up to anyone, even if you know there's going to be some backlash.

## Make people respect and value your time

Your time on this planet is very short, and it's extremely valuable. As part of standing up for yourself, you have to make sure that the people in your life realize that. If someone shows no respect for your time, then you have to cut the amount of time you give to them.

## Ensure that you always stay calm when you confront manipulators

You'll come up with a strategy to assert for yourself, but no matter how well thought out your plan is, it could fail if you let emotions get in the way. The only way to win is by staying calm. When you confront a controlling person, make sure that you process the entire interaction through the logical part of your brain, not the emotional part.

This is going to be difficult; as we have already mentioned in the book, emotions are more primal than logic, so it's very easy for them to take over. You have to make a concerted effort to stay calm and logical.

When you stand up to someone, emotion is your enemy; it doesn't matter if it's a positive emotion or a negative one; it's going to work against you. When controlling people see that you are finally standing up to them, they'll react in an emotional way.

Emotions can be infectious (for example, when someone raises their voice in a conversation, you will instinctively do the same) but you have to make a mental effort not to mirror the manipulators' emotions. Make your point in a calm voice, and if they react with anger, let them vent, then reiterate your point calmly as you address any points they may have raised in their angry tirade.

You may feel strong emotions in the process, and you'll definitely be tempted to act on those emotions, but at that moment, you should realize that the stakes are much higher than that; you are trying to regain control over your life, and emotions are of no use for you at that moment. Unless you control your emotions, you won't be able to regain control over your life.

## Have specific expectations when confronting controlling people

When a controlling person demands something of you, and you choose to stand up to them, you are going to have a pivotal conversation with them. You should only go into that conversation with a definite set of expectations; without clear expectations, there is no way to gauge whether or not you have succeeded in getting what you want.

That means you have to plan. Your plan can be something like "By the end of the conversation, I want him to understand that I won't put up with his verbal abuses." During the conversation, when you notice that the controlling person is trying to digress, you should keep turning the conversation back on course, and don't fall into his trap and forget what subject you are trying to address.

When you are done talking to him, based on his responses, you will be able to tell whether you have succeeded in getting your message across to him. If he raises a different issue that you care about, don't fall for it. Make sure that the conversation is about something specific, not a highlight of all the issues that ail your relationship.

When the controlling person brings up something else, tell him, "That is a topic for another day. At this moment we are addressing this topic". When you are trying to regain control over your life, it's more effective to conclusively address one topic at a time, instead of opening up multiple wounds and creating confusion. Manipulators thrive when there is confusion in the air, so don't give them the upper hand.

**Be patient**

As you stand up for yourself, you have to remember that you are overhauling your entire behavioral pattern. The people who have taken over your life have come to expect you to be agreeable. When you push back and demand to be treated fairly, they probably won't take you seriously at first.

They are going to ignore what you have told them, and they'll resort to treating you the same way they have always done. They are hoping that your new-found confidence is just a temporary thing and that soon, things will go back to "normal." So, when at first, you notice that people aren't taking you seriously, you have to be patient and to keep demanding the respect and the consideration that you know you deserve.

If you raise an issue with a manipulative person today, and the next day, he violates your new agreed-upon terms, don't let it slide. If you threatened certain consequence, make sure that you follow through. The hardest part of standing up for yourself will be proving to the people who are used to walking all over you that you actually mean what you say. So, don't give up on your stand at first sight of resistance.

**Ensure that you are transparent**

Many victims try to stand up for themselves but fail in doing so. Often times, it's because they fail to be both transparent and authentic. Manipulative people choose to target people who worry too much about how others feel because they have a hard time expressing their true feeling because they want to avoid being offensive.

Controlling people fully expect that their victims will confront them at some point, but they are always counting on the fact that the victims will tiptoe around the core issues rather than addressing them head-on. When the victim tiptoes around an issue out of fear that he or she is going to offend the manipulator's sensibilities, that gives the manipulator the power to interpret the confrontation however they like, and they are very good at justifying their oppressive tendencies and finding loopholes in social contracts.

When you stand up for yourself, don't assume that there is anything that should "go without saying." You have already established that the manipulative person is not a rational actor, so don't lie to yourself or pretend that they'll be considerate to you out of the goodness of their own hearts. If you want them to stop acting in a certain way, make sure that you state it out loud, in no uncertain terms. Make sure that you address all your concerns head-on, and that there is absolutely no room for misunderstanding or ambiguity.

## Don't worry about coming across as selfish

The fear of being perceived as selfish is the main reason why people voluntarily choose to put the needs of others before their own, even if they destroy their lives in the process. When you stand up for yourself, the manipulative person may counter by accusing you of selfishness, or you may even feel a bit guilty on your own (because of the value system that you have).

Here is the news flash for you: Manipulative people are themselves selfish. In fact, they take selfishness to a whole other level; not only do they serve their own interests, but they also use others to serve their interests – that is about as selfish as one can get.

So, when you confront a manipulative person, no matter how selfish you sound, you are nowhere close to that person's level of selfishness – that means you should be secure in your conviction that you need to assert for yourself.

## Timing is important

You should carefully choose the time when you want to stand up to a manipulative person. You might be tempted to stand up to the person in the heat of the moment, but that's not always a good idea; emotions might cloud your judgment, and you might not properly articulate the point you are trying to make. You are better off conversing with the person at a time when everyone is calm and collected.

If the manipulative person asks you to do something and you want to say "No" but you can't think of the right way to say it, you might be better off telling him to let you think about it for a while so that you can get back to him. He might try to push you to give an immediate answer. If he does this, then you have no choice but to say "No," and if he demands an explanation, you can always tell him that it's too big a thing to take on without taking time to consider it.

## Be ready for the backlash

There is nothing more terrifying to a controlling person that the feeling that he or she is losing control over someone. These people spend a lot of time and energy, manipulating others so that they can dominate them, and when they see their victims become empowered, it frightens them, and they'll react in a drastic way, hoping to retain that control.

Manipulators are also used to getting what they want, so when they realize that this won't be the case anymore, their reaction will be dire. So, when you defend against such people, there is one thing that you can always count on; backlash!

You have to figure out what the "worst-case scenario" could be based on what you know about the manipulator, and you need to prepare for that scenario. Often times, the person may use an extreme version of his most favorite manipulation technique to keep you from slipping away from his or her control.

If he likes to guilt trip you, he will deploy the mother of all guilt-trips. If he likes to shame you, he will use the most shameful thing he can think of. If he likes to intimidate you, he will bring up the scenario that you fear the most. Be mentally prepared for this.

If you sense that he might be a person who's likely to resort of physical violence, try to stand up to him in a public place such as a restaurant, where there are going to be witnesses should he try something violent.

If you sense that it's a person who likes to "play the victim," it might also be useful to have some witnesses around. Try to control the environment where you choose to confront the controlling person so that when the backlash inevitably comes, the person is unable to act out on his worst impulses.

# Conclusion

I hope you have learned valuable information that will help you stay vigilant and protect yourself against the machinations of the manipulative and controlling people that you encounter in all walks of life.

The next step is to start reviewing all of your relationships and figuring out whether they are tainted by any of the manipulation techniques that we have talked about in this book. To have relationships that are truly healthy and beneficial to you, it's important to make sure that they are not based on manipulation.

You might have settled into certain habits or patterns with your partner, family members, friends, and colleagues, without even realizing that you were emotionally exploited. As you review those dynamics, identify any areas where you feel emotionally shortchanged, and use what you have learned here to rectify the situations.

From this point on, you have to learn to stand up for yourself in order to defeat the manipulative agendas of others. Don't let anyone manipulate you by victimizing you, playing with your emotions, lying to you, using your weaknesses against you, or even by smothering you with affection.

Even though we have looked at the dark aspects of human nature in this book, it's important for you to remember that people are generally good, so don't close yourself off to new experiences out of fear of being manipulated. You can have happy and healthy relationships with people if you encourage them to join you on your journey to emotional maturity.

Finally, if you found this book at all useful, a review on Amazon will be greatly appreciated!